THE CIRCUMSTANCE OF THE SYSTEM

RICK BULLARD

Dedicated to anyone who ever felt out of place in the world they were told to accept.

If you've ever thought, "This can't be all there is," you're not alone.

Contents

Prologue

The System

We were born into it, raised by it, shaped by it, and told it was "freedom"… and I've always had a problem with that for as far back as I can remember. Not the freedom part, but the lie behind it.

The walls of this system are made up of habits and rules, traditions, expectations, and a thousand little transactions you didn't agree to and yet still have to obey. You've been trained to navigate through it so well that you don't even notice the walls around you anymore. You've become comfortable in them.

And that, my friend, as you will see… is the problem.

The System isn't just a single walled structure, though. It's a legion of sub-systems and other structures that mesh together, which you'll soon come to know and understand much better as you continue reading.

I'll discuss things like the economy that decides your

worth. The politics that have you fighting against your neighbor. The religion that claims ownership over your soul. The schools that teach obedience instead of thought. The media that sells you a version of reality shaped to fit the agenda of those who own it. And the quiet "social contracts" that tell you who you can and can't be without ever having signed any documents.

If you try to pull away from The System too much, it has ways to push you back in. Laws, fines, fear, ridicule, and the simple threat of losing what little stability you've been allowed. It doesn't need to kill you to keep you compliant. It just needs you tired, distracted, and grateful for the scraps you occasionally receive from it.

This isn't conspiracy that I'll be talking about in this book. It's infrastructure. And it's not hiding in the shadows anymore. It's hiding right here, in plain sight.

The System isn't some distant machine in a hidden room somewhere. It's seen in the price of your groceries, the length of your workweek, the content of your news feed, and in the many other "life options" you think you get to choose on your own.

Many people are already waking up and beginning to see the flaws in it all. Not because the system is weakening, but because more and more people are starting to see the shape of the walls, or should I say, cage that's around them. Once you finally see it for what it is, you begin to look beyond it. You start noticing the patterns in it. The repetition that it brings. The quiet recursion of control disguised as progress.

That's what this book is about.

It's not about the systems you've been taught to fear so much as the ones you've been taught to trust. And if you read this book all the way through, you might not look at your life, or the world, the same way again.

At least, that's my hope for you.

The darkness of The System can be overwhelming at times, so I recommend reading only a few chapters at a time. I don't speak much about the benefits of The System in this book, mostly because they're so few and far between.

But, when you make it to the latter chapters, you'll notice that I present an alternative system for you. Along with the baby steps that you can take at the end of each chapter that have been labeled "So What Now?" which will help you make little adjustments to your life along the way. When you arrive at the final page, you'll have the ability to not only see the current system for the detriment that it is, but you'll also find an opening that you can just barely squeeze through to find the light on the other side and keep moving.

Welcome to **The Circumstance of the System**.

Now let's tear this thing apart…

Chapter 1

The Grind

You woke up this morning to an alarm you didn't want to hear, at a time you didn't choose yourself, for a job you wouldn't do if you weren't being forced to do it, so that you can pay your rent, your debt, and the other expenses that come with trying to survive in this world.

By the time your feet hit the floor, you're already behind. You move through the same rooms, in the same order, every workday, on autopilot.

Shower. Clothes. Coffee. Keys. Traffic. Or some variation of those movements with maybe a little bite to eat in there somewhere to give you the energy you'll need to get through the first segment of your workday. You then trade hours of your life for paper currency, and then, at the end of the week, you hand that currency right back to someone else to keep a roof over your head, food on the table, lights to see by, water to wash with, gas to cook with, and whatever other scraps of distraction you can afford so that you don't go insane.

You call it "making a living," but it feels a lot more like you're renting out your own existence, doesn't it?

You tell yourself, "this is just how things are. Everyone else is doing it, right?" So, you grind your day away, you earn your money, and you do your best to survive.

But The Grind isn't the *natural* cost of living your life. It's just the tax you pay for existing in someone else's system. And we've built it so well, that most people will defend the damn thing like it's sacred!

You tend to dress it up with words like "hustle," and "responsibility." You come up with slogans to make the cage feel noble. Phrases like, "Hard work pays off," "You'll thank yourself later." But later never comes, because "later" is the bait. And you're already on the hook.

Work itself isn't the problem, really. There are moments when your work actually gives you pride, like when you finish a task and feel like it mattered a great deal to someone, when a paycheck means your family eats well that day or that week, or when you walk away from a day feeling accomplished. Those moments are important, and I'm not trying to take those away from you. But the system takes that honest goodness that you're doing and it twists it until it feels like survival is the only reward left.

Look at the trades you make each day: your health, your energy, your time; most of it with people you don't even like, in exchange for just enough comfort to keep you from rebelling against it all.

You hear people say that "rest is a luxury, not a right." You're told that free time is something you have to earn. You're taught to feel guilty for stopping. And *that alone* should tell you that this isn't about thriving, but about compliance.

And even if you play it all perfectly… you show up early, stay late, hit every target… the system will still keep you one missed paycheck away from collapse! Because that's the point of it all. The "owners" don't want you to be secure. They want you to be compliant and struggling just enough to always need them.

Along with the physical exhaustion that you constantly feel also comes the mental erosion. Your spark begins to fade, your reactions begin to dull. You scroll through the screen at night, not because you care about what's on the screen so much, but because your brain can't find the energy to do anything else.

When someone asks you how you're doing, you say "fine," because explaining the truth would take far too much effort. But that's not "fine." That's the sound of your inner life being snuffed out.

We call all of this "maturity," "responsibility," "adulthood." But most of the time, it's nothing more than surrender. You hand over years of your life in exchange for survival, and you call that "success" because calling it what it really is… is even worse.

And the damage doesn't stop with you…

Entire families get hollowed out by The Grind. Parents become ghosts in their own homes, their bodies present but their minds are trapped in the next job or deadline. Marriages become stretched thin by schedules and bills. Friendships become "someday" promises that never come to fruition. Joy becomes nostalgia, like something you talk about in past-tense instead of actually living. The Grind doesn't just take your time. It steals your *presence*, then it convinces you that you never had it to begin with.

Some even have a twisted sense of pride in being worn down by it all. They like to brag about their sixty-hour workweeks, or about never taking a vacation. Like suffering in this way is a badge of honor. But it's not a damn badge! And there's absolutely no honor in working your life into the ground!

Yet you're still told to be grateful for it all, aren't you? Grateful for the job, even if it's killing you. Grateful for the roof over your head, even if the stress of keeping it up is too much to manage. Grateful for the food you eat, even if the poisons in it are slowly killing you.

Gratitude is great when it's honest. But when it's a gag in your mouth, it's just another way to keep you quiet. You can be thankful for everything and still tell the truth: this system doesn't care how hard you work. It just wants you to keep working.

If you're Gen X like me, you've watched The Grind change shape for each generation it consumes, but it keeps bearing the same claws each time around.

We were the latchkey kids, learning "independence"

with a side of neglect. We did what we had to do to survive. The Millennial generation got sold a bill of goods about education and opportunity, only to get slammed with debt and a job market designed to bleed them slowly. Then Gen Z came up inside "The Feed," already juggling side hustles before they finished high school, and having to compete with algorithms for relevance. And heaven only knows what Generation Alpha and beyond will have to suffer from in the future!

But it's all the same machine every time. It's always the same race to nowhere. Only, it's getting worse with each decade that passes as inflation continues to rise and wages remain stagnant.

This is a model that wasn't built for most humans to thrive in, but for markets to extract from. And when you eventually see that, you finally stop blaming yourself for being so tired all the time.

See, The Grind is a cultural phenomenon that's been engineered, and is maintained this way on purpose.

And one thing's for certain…

This is not how life should feel.

At all!

So What Now?

What do you do when you realize the game is rigged?

You stop playing it, right?

You stop glorifying exhaustion like it's a badge of honor.

You stop giving The Grind more than it deserves.

Start with the smallest rebellion: protect your time like it's yours. Because it is!

Say no when the boss asks you to work weekends.

Take breaks without apology.

Put effort into what actually feeds your soul, not just what pays someone else.

Stop waiting for "someday" to arrive.

Someday isn't coming.

But today—this moment right here—is what you have.

So, take back your life, piece by piece.

Chapter 2

The Trade

There's no freedom to be an individual in this system.

We're told to "be yourself," to "live your truth," but only if that truth doesn't mess with someone else's profit margin, and only if your path still fits inside someone else's schedule.

Sure, you're allowed to be different...but not too different, as I've had to learn the hard way. You can't be disruptive and speaking out on things that really matter in this world. You can't be inconvenient by shaking people up with the truth. The moment your authenticity starts to threaten the system's structure, you'll find out exactly how conditional that "freedom" you thought you had really is!

But from day one, you're directed straight into the system. You're told to pick something stable, something smart, or something that looks good on paper, even if it feels wrong in your bones. Your life gets mapped out according to someone else's fears and standards. Then you're expected to be grateful for whatever it is you've been handed. You're expected to make it work, even if every step you take sends you further away from who you are as an individual.

By the time you're old enough to want something different, or something that feeds your soul, the trap's already been set. The bills have started rolling in, and the debt's already piling up. You've got responsibilities now, and changing directions at this point suddenly feels like you're being reckless. So, what do you do? You stay where you are and you push down your instincts. You numb the ache in your chest and you tell yourself that this is what being a "grown-up" looks like. But deep down, you know you've traded something off somewhere, but you can't quite name what that was anymore.

What you *really* want is that freedom I mentioned earlier.

Well… good luck with that.

Try telling your boss you need more time for yourself. Try telling the bank you can't make your mortgage payment because you need to prioritize your mental health right now. Try telling your parents you're not interested in chasing the same version of success that they follow. Watch how fast the room goes silent.

This world doesn't reward presence. It rewards productivity. It doesn't value peace the way it should, either. It only values performance.

So, what do you do about it?

Nothing.

You step into the cage every morning at 9 a.m., and at 5 p.m., you step back out. You go home, where you try to feel something after being locked away all day, and then prepare to walk into the cage again tomorrow.

That's The Trade. You give your energy, your ideas, your time, your attention, your presence, and in return, you get little scraps of green paper for all of it. Not enough to change anything. Just enough to keep you coming back for more.

Most of the time, you don't even know that you're trading your life away until years of it have gone by. You just voluntarily submit to it because "that's just the way it is," right?

The system is so subtle in its tyranny. It doesn't rip freedom away from you all at once; it chips it away slowly. With routine, and structure. Until eventually, you look around and realize you haven't made a truly free decision for yourself in years.

You start missing the point of your own life and calling it being responsible. You stop seeing your family and calling it providing. You give up your time, your creativity, your instincts, and your identity, and they call it being "a good worker." But being a good worker and being a good human are not the same thing. And more often than not, the better you get at one, the further you drift away from being the other.

You're not just trading your time for money. You're

trading your presence for approval, your sense of self for the illusion of stability. And the system makes you feel guilty when you notice it. Like the moment you speak up about how empty it all feels, you're betraying something sacred. This is when everyone around you freaks out over your betrayal of systemic oppression! But you're not betraying anything! You're just waking up. And the people around you who are still asleep won't like that at all... because your clarity threatens their comfort.

We're not just talking about your "job," here. This is about how we've structured *life itself*. It's about a way of living that convinces you to sacrifice your joy for status, your time for an image, your soul for a paycheck, and then has the audacity to tell you that you're the selfish one if you decide to no longer play along.

We've been sold a script from the very beginning. Go to school, get a degree, pick a career, take out a loan, work hard, get a mortgage, get married, have kids, and then retire when you're too old to enjoy life. But the truth is, for many of us, that script ends early on with debt, disconnection, and dreams that never got to see the light of day. And if you try to deviate from the script... if you say, "Maybe this doesn't work for me" You get ostracized by family, friends and coworkers, and then you're branded a disappointment. As if choosing a life you think that you'll enjoy makes you a coward or something.

If you're a man, it's even more layered. We're raised to tie our value to usefulness. If you're not providing, you're failing your loved ones. If you're not producing, you're lazy. And rest? Forget about that! Rest is for the weaklings! Vulnerability? That's for the pansies. So we have to grind our lives away, we have to shut up, stuff it all down and pretend everything's fine. And eventually, we forget how to even access the parts of ourselves that aren't wrapped up in proving something to everyone else.

No wonder so many men wake up in a mid-life crisis, wondering who the hell they even are anymore!

But most of us didn't choose this life. I know I didn't. We just woke up in it. And by the time we realized what we were giving up, we were already neck-deep in it all…

All of the obligations, the debt, the schedules, and the pressure. It all kept us from saying; "This doesn't feel right!" Because you realize the minute that you do, you'll just be told to get back to work…like the slave that you really are.

Silence is how the system stays alive. It doesn't continue on through violence or outright threats. It exists through anxiety and exhaustion. You're too busy to question it, too tired and anxious, and too worried about surviving to risk anything. So you keep making The Trade. Day after day. Year after year. And somewhere in the quiet moments between all the bullshit you put up with, you feel that dull ache of something slipping away. Something essential. Something you can't name but desperately want to get back. Like that freedom you had when you were a kid.

Remember that?

You're not crazy for wanting it back. You're not

ungrateful for questioning all of this. You're not selfish for wanting your life to feel like you own it. You're waking up in a world full of sleepers. And that alone is the first act of rebellion in a world that trains you to forget yourself.

See, if we're not careful, though, we'll keep walking into that cage every morning until we finally forget what freedom ever felt like.

…and that's when The Trade is complete.

So What Now?

Stop entering the cage every morning without thinking.

Start carving out time that's actually yours.

Stop saying yes to everything just to keep the peace.

Build something—anything—that isn't tied to their leash.

A skill. A side hustle. A small habit of your own making. Something that reminds you that your life belongs to you. Something that you actually enjoy.

You don't have to ask permission to exist on your own terms. You just have to want it bad enough to stop caring what other people think.

Your life isn't a service contract.

Rip that damn thing up!

Chapter 3

The Clock

We act like time belongs to us. Like we own it, and we can manage it, schedule it, and bend it to our will. But most people don't actually own any of their time at all. They rent it out to the system. Hour by hour. Week by week. Month after month. Year after year. And if they're lucky enough, they get just a few scattered hours back here and there, but only after they've given their best ones away.

The problem is, when you finally get those scraps of time, those late nights when your mind is already fried, or those weekends that vanish under all the errands and exhaustion, it doesn't feel like "free time" at all, does it? Not really. It feels more like an afterthought. Like time you're supposed to squeeze meaning out of, even though there's nothing left in the tank. So you sit there staring at your computer, or the TV, trying to convince yourself that you're "relaxing." But you're not really relaxing, are you? No, you're just recovering and recalibrating just enough to do it all over again on the next work day.

We're raised on clocks and taught to live by them and obey them. Hell, I'd even say we worship them to some degree! School bells, lunch breaks, shift changes, reminders, alarms. Even as little kids, time isn't something we feel, it's something we follow. Something that dictates when we can speak, eat, leave, or rest. And by adulthood, most people don't even question this structure at all.

When you clock in each day, you're not just showing up for work, you're signing over minutes and hours of your life. And for every one that you give to them, you're losing one that could've gone towards *anything* else.

But we don't ask ourselves what our time here is *really* worth. We just accept the numbers that they give us. $15 an hour. $35 if you're lucky. And we build our entire lives around it. We arrange our schedules, our energy, our self-worth around what The Clock allows. We wake up at this time, eat at this time, leave by this time, sleep when it's socially acceptable, and then repeat it over and over until you stop noticing how artificial it all feels.

Even our downtime is scheduled. Our connections are squeezed into windows of time. Dinner gets a time slot, and our hobbies have to be written in on the calendar. We book our vacations months in advance and then spend half the time checking our phones anyway. And when it's all over, we return to The Clock like nothing happened. You don't feel rested at all, you just feel *delayed*. Like you fell behind for even daring to pause for yourself.

And that's the part that really messes with your head, isn't it? You start feeling guilty for resting, for slowing down a bit, for not being "productive enough."

We talk about "free time" like it's some noble concept, but time isn't free if it comes at the cost of your nervous system and your sanity. It's not free if you have to dig yourself out of a backlog just to enjoy it. And it sure as hell isn't free if you spend it trying to numb yourself so you don't feel how fast it's all slipping away.

And yet we measure everything in increments of time now… Steps, sleep cycles, screen time, heart rates. Even time with our kids has become something we track and optimize. "Fifteen quality minutes a day." That's how disconnected we've become. Time has turned from an experience with our loved ones into a calculation. A mere ledger of usefulness. And in many cases, if something doesn't produce a result, it's seen as waste.

This system wants you to stay busy. Always. It wants every idle second of your life filled. Scroll, swipe, watch, hustle. It doesn't care if you're fulfilled; it only cares that you're engaged. It only cares that your time, even your downtime, still feeds the machine.

You can't sit still without feeling like you're falling behind. You can't rest without guilt gnawing on your brain. You're trained to feel shame the second you're not producing something. And that's not a personal flaw. It's really not your fault at all! That's the systems programming. You're not anxious about time because you're lazy. You're anxious because the second you're not feeding the machine, it makes you feel like you don't exist.

If you've ever sat in a quiet room and couldn't relax, even though you were desperate for peace... that's exactly what I'm talking about!

But the damage that all of this does isn't just physical. It's also spiritual, emotional. *Existential.* We've become so disconnected from the natural rhythm of nature that we don't even know how to recognize it anymore. We think we're lazy when we rest. We think we're wasting time when we sit in stillness. But maybe that's not the problem at all. Maybe the problem is we've been sold a version of time that doesn't really exist.

Real time...the kind that fills you up instead of draining you, doesn't come with a clock. It comes with *presence*, like when you lose yourself in something meaningful. When hours pass like minutes because your soul is actually engaged. But how often do we get that anymore? How often are we truly in that space? Not thinking about the next task, not waiting for the moment to end, but fully inside it?

Rarely, right?

Because that kind of time doesn't always make the green paper for you, does it? So it feels wasted.

And if you're thinking, "Well, that's just how the world works," then that's proof of how deep the conditioning runs in you.

We act like this was the only way that things could've gone. But time didn't always feel like this. There was an age when people owned their lives and their time. When community dictated rhythm more than corporate calendars. When seasons mattered more than schedules. When we rose with the sun and slept when we were tired. When life itself dictated time… instead of deadlines.

But now, even our children are on clocks. Homework, testing, extracurricular activities, and bedtime routines optimized for the parents' morning and evening rush. We condition them early. And then, when they grow up anxious, disconnected, and exhausted, we act surprised by it. But it's not surprising at all! It's actually predictable if you could just realize what you've been doing all this time.

We built it this way!

And somewhere deep in your gut, you know it. That tension in your chest. That racing mind at 2 a.m. keeping you awake. That constant feeling that no matter what you do, it's never enough. That's not you. That's The Clock owning you.

You were never supposed to *earn* rest. You were supposed to live a life where rest was integrated, and time flowed with you, not against you. But in this structure, in this system, everything is inverted. Slowness equals laziness. Stillness equals failure. Fatigue equals weakness. And the only way to be worthy is to be constantly busy… and tired.

But the more time you sell, or give away, the less of it you actually feel. And the longer you do it, the harder it becomes to remember what your time even felt like before they put a price tag on it.

Time was never supposed to feel like this.

So What Now?

Well, they obviously don't just steal your time, they sell it back to you. But make no mistake: Every minute you take back is a mutiny.

So steal it, and guard it! Rip it out of their hands if you have to. Say no to the meeting. Ignore the guilt and let the world wait for once.

Because time isn't just a resource.

It's your fucking life!

And if they've convinced you that you have to earn your own existence…

Then every second you reclaim is a middle finger to the machine!

Chapter 4

The Disconnect

You know…most of us aren't really living. We're simply acting. Playing out roles that we never auditioned for in a world that doesn't care who we are beneath the surface. All of the fake smiles we present to the world daily, the nods we give to higher ups in meetings, and the laughter at "jokes" that we know aren't really funny. It's all been carefully filtered by us to pass as "normal." But underneath that facade, we're all just numb. Exhausted, really. We're split down the middle between who we are and who we're expected to be.

That split is what I call The Disconnect.

And it's so common now, we treat it like it's personality.

You can spot it in people's eyes if you look close enough. They have that glazed over, distant look that says, "I'm here… but just barely." That tone they have when they say they're "doing fine." Or maybe it's that twitch of anxiety when they sit still for more than five minutes.

See, no one taught them how to *feel*. They were only taught how to *perform*. So now, when the real emotions show up inside—grief, happiness, anger, disgust—they don't know what the hell to do with any of it!

We've been raised to function…instead of exist.

This system doesn't just demand your time as we discussed in the previous chapter. It demands your *identity*. And if you don't hand it over willingly, it'll take it in pieces. First it takes your voice, by silencing you. Then it takes the little things that made you different from everyone else. Until eventually, what's left is a version of you that's easy to market and schedule. You'll still get to be mostly you, but just a version that's been watered down so much that no one will notice who you *really* are.

What most people don't realize about themselves is that, instead of waking up, they tend to double down and start drowning everything out with what I call "noise." With more work, more screens, more scrolling, more distractions, or more drugs and alcohol. Because silence is dangerous when you're disconnected. In silence, the truth gets louder. And the truth is, most people don't even know what the truth is anymore! They only know what they're allowed to know. So, the silence is oppressive to them.

And that's just sad…

You were never meant to lose your instincts. You were never meant to second-guess your own joy, your own ideas, your own damn voice! But when you're constantly being told who to be—by ads, by school, by family, by everyone trying to sell you a better version of yourself—you start to think the real you isn't good enough. Or worse… it isn't even real!

So, people settle for jobs that drain them, relationships that dull them, lives that don't resemble anything they ever dreamed of.

But hey, at least it looks fine from the outside, right? That's the gold standard now. As long as you look good, you must be fine. Just say the right things, keep busy, don't ask any questions and you're good to go.

But what happens when the mask you're wearing starts to come apart? What happens when you can't keep up the performance anymore? That's when the real fear sets in, isn't it? Because if you've spent your entire life being who you were supposed to be, then who the hell are you when that version stops working?

Think about *that* for a while…

No one talks about that identity crisis. About the slow, choking grief of realizing you've never really known yourself. And the system sure as hell doesn't want you to talk about it! Because if enough people did, it might all start to unravel overnight. You might stop buying what they're selling, chasing what they've told you mattered, or stop playing along with their rigged game altogether.

That's why this emotional suppression is baked into everything. You're praised for keeping it together. For being strong, and staying positive. But ask yourself this:

who does your "strength" benefit? Because if your ability to stay numb keeps the machine running, maybe it's not strength at all. Maybe it's just you quietly surrendering.

It comes in all forms too…

The man who hasn't cried in years and calls it "discipline." The kid who gave up asking "why" after years of being told to sit down and shut up. The artist who put down the brush because there was no time left for creativity after work. The friend who stopped calling because every conversation felt like it was fake. These aren't personal flaws in people. These are systemic amputations. Bits of our selves, cut off for the sake of survival.

We give all of this labels like "burnout." "Depression." "Disconnection." But really, it's just the logical outcome of a culture that rewards conformity and calls emotion a liability. The more you actually feel, the more inconvenient you are to it all. The more you care, the more exhausted you become. And the more awake you are, the more alienated you'll be.

It's a vicious cycle.

You ever sit in your car and feel like you're about to scream but don't even know why?

Ever feel like your whole life you've been running, but you're not sure what you're running from (or to)?

Those are normal responses to a life that never gave

you time to figure out who the hell you even are!

You've been playing roles for so long you forgot who's number one.

That's The Disconnect.

And no, it's not going to fix itself. Because the system isn't going to hand you back your identity with an apology. It's going to just keep demanding more. More of your attention, your time, your energy, and definitely more of your silence.

And it'll keep draining you… until you decide you've had enough.

You want to reconnect? Then stop pretending everything's fine! Stop calling numbness "normal," or shrinking your voice just to fit in.

The system didn't bury the real you.

You did!

Because it taught you that hiding was safer than being seen.

But hiding is not going to save you.

Reclaiming yourself will.

So What Now?

Start with one brutal question:

"Who am I when no one's watching?"

If you don't know the answer, you've got work to do. I'm not talking about the kind that pleases your boss, or the kind that earns applause or money, but the kind that digs deep and looks carefully at the conditioning you've endured.

Turn off the noise. Feel the damn feelings. Rage. Cry. Sit in silence. Get uncomfortable. Then start reclaiming the pieces of yourself.

Say what you actually mean for once! Quit performing for people who wouldn't notice if you vanished. Make art. Break those routines. Get weird. Go outside and dance in the rain. Stop explaining yourself for doing things that make you feel like **you**.

And for the love of whatever's left of you…don't wait for permission!

You've already lost too much of yourself waiting around. The real you is still in there, buried under all the masks the system sewed to your face.

What are you waiting for?

Go in and get them out!

Chapter 5

The Paper

Money runs everything in this world.

It alone is one of the worst constructs that we as humans ever brought into existence.

It doesn't matter how kind, creative, skilled, or driven you are, if you don't have money, the world treats you like you don't matter.

I learned this very early on in life.

It's the one system you can't opt out of. You can question religion, ignore politics, never go to the doctor, but you can't live without money! And you know what I find crazy about it all? It's not because life itself *requires* money... but because we've made it so that it does!

The monetary system wasn't created to empower people, it was made to control them. And that control works best when people are always just a little bit desperate. When you're barely keeping your head above water, you don't have time to think, create, challenge, or dream. You're too busy *surviving* to notice that you're being screwed by the system.

People will say, "Oh yeah, but hard work will make you rich!" Okay, but if that were true, construction and field workers would all be millionaires by now!

It's funny how the people breaking their backs are usually the ones with the least to show for it. Meanwhile, the people profiting the most are sitting on inherited wealth, passive income, and tax breaks the rest of us will never qualify for.

We all know that the game is rigged and has never been fair. But what's worse than that is… it was never meant to be!

See, they (those who already have money) don't want you to be wealthy. They just want you *chasing* wealth. They don't want you to be completely free, either. They just want you *hoping* for freedom. Because hope keeps you compliant, and desperation keeps you quiet.

When you mention how difficult it is to get by from week to week, they'll say you should budget better, work harder, hustle more. Take side jobs. Get a certification. Be more marketable. Start a business…

But no one wants to talk about the real issue here:

The cost of living has been rigged to rise faster than your ability to keep up! It doesn't matter how smart you are, or how hard you work… if the rent, groceries, and gas prices keep climbing while your wage stays frozen in place, you're on a fucking hamster wheel!

When you do finally break down and start complaining about the unfairness of it all, they hit you with shame. "You should've saved more." "You should've invested." "You should've made better money choices." As if this system teaches that, or even leaves room for it! As if the average person isn't already doing mental gymnastics just to keep their damn lights on!

But, scarcity is profitable for these entitled pricks! When people are scared of losing everything they own, they'll accept almost anything; like low wages, poor living conditions, toxic jobs, all the way down to total burnout.

It's a never ending struggle.

Fear makes you easy to manage. And the fear of going broke and losing everything you have is the leash they use to keep you pulling you back in.

They want you stuck. They want you to feel like your self-worth is tied to your net worth. Because people who feel inadequate will keep producing just to feel worthy.

Meanwhile, they glamorize wealth all around you. Flash it on the screens in front of your face. Sell you self-help courses to make you think it's just a mindset issue. They'll say, "You're not rich because you're not manifesting hard enough." What a convenient lie for the people who already own everything!

You can visualize all you want, but try paying your rent or mortgage with positive energy and let me know how that goes!

We've turned life into a subscription model. Pay to exist. Pay to eat. Pay to sleep indoors. Miss a payment? You're out. No dignity. No reprieve. Just out on the streets just like that!

And we've normalized this bullshit! We've accepted that *existing* comes with monthly fees!

…I'll never understand it.

But while we're on this topic, let's not forget about the system's favorite shackle...

Debt.

From student loans to credit cards to payday traps, debt is how the system keep you tied to a future you never even considered. You start your life off already behind and then you spend the rest of your life trying to catch up. What's funny is the system creates the cost involved, then it offers you the credit to cover it. Now they've got you trapped coming and going! Interest. Fees. Threats. Stress. Obedience.

That's what most people call "life" now.

But the thing that very few people will acknowledge about all of this is that *money* is the sickness! It's one of the worst ideas humanity ever agreed on. We invented it, then we let it own us. It didn't just corrupt the system; it *became* the system! It divides people by worth. Pits neighbor against neighbor. It pressures, isolates, and dehumanizes. It makes people value numbers more than each other. And the sickest part is that we've been trained to believe that this is the best that we can do. That charging people for resources, natural to our world, is somehow logical.

That struggling for scraps while billionaires hoard those same resources is just how the world works.

Do you *actually believe* that bullshit?

It's how you're kept broke and trained to chase money instead of questioning the system that makes you need so much of it. It's why you feel like you're failing when in reality, the system is succeeding at what it was made to do: Keep you too busy earning a living to ever create a damn life!

So What Now?

Stop treating The Paper like it's your master.

Start treating it like it's your enemy in disguise.

Use money only as a tool, never as a measure of worth. Starve the system that starves you back. Spend only where your values live.

Shop local.

Invest in people, not products.

And if the price of something is more than you can manage, walk the hell away!

You don't need **more** paper.

You need **less** chains.

Chapter 6

The Puppet Show

Politics is the most effective illusion of freedom ever created. It's the system's way of convincing people that they have power and representation, when in reality, they're just watching a rigged game play out from the bleachers.

Every four years you're told to vote like your life depends on it, as if choosing which puppet wears the suit this time is the same thing as having control over what that suit actually does. No matter who gets elected each cycle, the working class keeps getting screwed, the rich keep getting richer, the wars are never ending, and the promises of a better society that they preach vanish as quickly as your hope does.

What we call "democracy" has been reduced to nothing more than a corporate loyalty program. Every few years, the public gets hyped up to choose their "team," as if that team isn't owned by the same donors as the other one.

It's all just theater.

The Puppet Show.

Two wings of the same bird of prey. You don't get *real* options in this system, you get pre-approved narratives wrapped in party colors and sold with assurances. Red, blue, conservative, liberal, progressive, patriot… it's all just tribal seduction! It keeps people fighting with each other instead of looking up and asking who the hell's actually representing whom.

But see, the rules of this game weren't written for you anyway. They were written *around* you. Around your labor, and your silence, around your desperation to believe that your voice still matters in a system that stopped listening to you a long time ago.

Sure, you can vote!

Big fucking deal!

Try running as an independent and see how fast the machine grinds you to dust. Try building momentum outside of the two-party framework and see how quickly your platform gets buried under red tape and media blackout. The system doesn't fear opposition! Hell, it *built* the opposition! It fears defection. It fears people who wake up and stop playing the damn game.

The parties pretend to hate each other, but at the very top, they're eating from the same plate. They play golf together. They invest in the same portfolios. They accept money from the same corporate sponsors and pass legislation that protects the wealthy, not the common people. They put on a show for the cameras, toss out buzzwords to rile up their base, and then get back to protecting their wealthy cohorts. That's their job, to keep the public distracted, divided, and just hopeful enough to keep voting. Meanwhile, the same problems persist. The same promises get recycled over and over and over again.

And the citizens keep getting steamrolled every single time.

But, you keep playing their game, so…what do you expect?

I often wonder how it's gone on for so long like this? It makes no sense to me that people would see it so clearly, and yet submit to it over and over again. Year after year. Getting so caught up in a single man or woman as their "savior" while he or she does absolutely *nothing* what-so-ever to free them from *anything!*

It's all misdirection. They hand you "enemies" to keep you from identifying the real threat. They say things like: Blame the immigrants. Blame the poor. Blame the people of color. Blame the liberals. Blame the conservatives. Blame the people who want too much. Blame the ones who don't want anything. Just don't blame the structure! Don't blame the unchecked power! And definitely don't blame the corporations writing legislation behind the scenes! Oh no! Don't do that!

That's the trick, see? Get the people angry, but keep

them misinformed. If you don't know who to fight, you end up fighting each other.

And they love to see you fight!

This is the part most people refuse to admit, but it's the truth none-the-less. You were never meant to win this! This process, this **voting** bullshit, was designed to wear you down and exhaust your hope. To make you feel like voting harder or yelling louder is the solution, when deep down, you know it isn't. You **know** it isn't! You've watched it play out what seems like a hundred times in your life. A new face, a fresh promise, a smooth tone. But somehow, the rich remain untouched, the wars never cease, the cost of living keeps rising, the corporations keep eating the planet. And nothing ever truly changes or even shifts…does it?

They shame you if you don't vote, though, as if participating in a scam gives you some moral high ground. As if your silence is the problem. It couldn't possibly be the system's complete and utter failure to respond to the people it claims to represent, could it?

But see, your silence can be a form of rebellion too. Sometimes not playing the game is the only honest move you have left. And as I've said before, the system doesn't want your voice; it wants your participation. It wants your consent. And when you stop giving it, they call you un-American.

See how that works?

We don't have a government anymore. We have a boardroom with flags around it. And the public aren't citizens anymore…we're data. Labor. PR statistics, and marketing leverage for politicians who build careers off pretending they understand the struggle. But the only thing they understand is power and money; how to gain it, how to keep it, and how to make sure you never get close to it.

They'll keep feeding you false hope every time. They'll tell you the system can be reformed from within.

HA!!

They say that if we just vote for the right person, everything will get better. Yeah, right.

"Change takes time"

But see, time is the one thing that most people no longer have. They're drowning in debt *now*. They're hungry *now*. They're losing their homes *now*.

Meanwhile, the laws keep stacking up to benefit the same people: the ones who already own everything. And when someone actually threatens that structure—calls out corruption, exposes fraud, demands accountability— they're labeled extremist. They're smeared. Censored. Silenced. The system doesn't tolerate truth that can't be monetized by them. And it doesn't reward integrity, either… it punishes it.

So, for once, stop lying to yourself. The rules were written to protect the power, not the people. They were written to appear fair while keeping the outcomes the same. They were written so you'd blame yourself for being exhausted, and for being fed up.

But the thing is… you're just living inside a machine that was never designed to serve you. It was designed to extract what it could *from you* and then discard you quietly when you stopped producing.

I'm not here to tell you who to vote for.

I'm here asking you why the hell you still believe that's even an option?

Do you really believe that any of these people actually represent you?

The longer you keep playing their game, the longer this system gets to keep pretending it was meant for you.

So What Now?

Stop picking a side.

Start choosing yourself as a representative of you and yours.

The next time someone tries to tell you the political system's broken, correct them. It's not broken at all. It's functioning perfectly for the people it was designed for. And the only way to stop being used by it is to stop playing by its rules.

Don't waste your breath defending your "team." Use it to call bullshit on the whole damn field.

No more voting for puppets.

Just walk away…

Chapter 7

The Pulpit

This is a touchy subject for some people, so I'll try to stay away from the spirituality aspect involved and focus solely on the system itself.

First off, religion was never meant to be a system to begin with. So it's kind of funny how it ended up making my list. But apparently, once man realized he could organize it, weaponize it, and monetize it, he did just that.

What should've been a personal connection to something greater, slowly over time became a chain of command. A man at the front of his "flock" with a book in his hand. The crowd below him, with their heads down. And just like that, the sacred got buried under rituals, rules, and a fear that shakes the very core of your being.

Let's be clear before we continue, this issue isn't about

a belief in a higher power. The issue is the structure that took that belief and turned it into a *business*. A hierarchy. A culture of obedience that's masked as "faith." A never-ending treadmill of guilt, shame, confession, and control. And people bought it hook, line and sinker, generation after generation, because they were told their eternity depended on it.

I'm sure that even many of you were told that questioning any of it meant that you had a lack of faith, right? That freedom from it all meant damnation for your soul. And that the only way to safely exist was under the watchful eye of the system itself.

The Pulpit doesn't care what you believe in your heart. It only cares if you follow the text that it hands you. It needs your participation, your service, your submission, and your fear-based loyalty. Because if people ever realized they didn't need a middleman to connect to the divine, the entire thing would collapse.

Think about that…

This system requires you to believe that you're broken by default, and it alone can fix you, but only after you've tithed, confessed, and sacrificed your instincts and handed over your authority.

It's not salvation!

It's a damn subscription!

It teaches you to distrust yourself. To second-guess your own conscience. To view your own desires, your own questions, even your doubts—not as human, but as sin.

That's just bullshit…

It doesn't guide you back to who you truly are. It teaches you to erase yourself in the name of something "greater." And when people falter under the weight of all that shame, what does the system do? It says, "pray harder," "have more faith," it says the problem is you, not the structure crushing you from the inside out.

Meanwhile, the ones who preach are protected from all of this, even though we can clearly see their *many* flaws. The ones who question the system are ostracized. And the ones who walk away are told they're lost, even if they've never felt more clear about these things in their lives.

Ask me how I know…

Let's stop pretending this is about holiness. It's always been about power. The power to control thought, behavior, and identity. To define right and wrong, and to dictate purpose, morality, and destiny. From a platform, from a book, and a man (or woman) behind a mic.

It's a system that was designed to keep people small. To hand them a mirror and convince them that they're filthy. Then sell them the soap to wash their filth away.

See, it's never been about connecting you to a God. It's been about making you believe you can't connect without *them*. Without their doctrine, their rituals, or their approval.

They build the maze and then offer to guide you through the maze… for a price. They gave you the fear of hell, and then sold you heaven. They defined your worth by how well you obey. They convinced you your body was a problem. That your thoughts were dangerous. That your questions were spiritual warfare. And you believed it, because they got to you early on in life.

They baptized you before you could even speak. They preached over your doubts before you knew what questions to ask. They told you that the world was fallen and they were your only way out.

That's not faith.

It's indoctrination.

And if you think that any of what I'm talking about stops at religion, you're not paying attention at all.

This kind of control bleeds into culture everywhere. Into politics, identity, how we raise our children, vote, love, and live.

Because once you train people to believe that they're broken and dependent… you can shape them into anything you want. And that's exactly what this system has done. It's turned purity into paranoia, sacrifice into self-destruction, worship into theater, and truth into whatever keeps the flock in line.

Somewhere along the way, religion stopped being a lifeline and became a leash. One that tightens the more you struggle to breathe on your own.

And just like the other systems I'll be talking about, it defends itself with the sharpest tools it has—fear, shame, and isolation.

Leave the church, and suddenly you're not just

doubting the pastor, you're betraying the universe. Speak out against it, and you're a heretic. Fall away, and they won't pray for you; they'll just gossip about you and then forget you.

You're not allowed to evolve.

You're not allowed to heal on your own.

You're only allowed to crawl back in and beg for forgiveness.

So What Now?

Don't just walk away from religion.

Wake up on your way out the door!

The truth isn't hiding under a steeple. It's already inside of you. You don't need a stage, a pulpit, or a priest to validate your worth. And you damn sure don't need a system to save you from yourself.

Ask the questions. Burn the scripts. You don't need their path to find your own.

Again… ask me how I know.

Chapter 8

The Bell

There's a reason they ring a bell to start and stop your school day.

The system has always wanted obedience, not originality. From the very beginning, school was designed to condition children for compliance. Sit down, raise your hand, speak only when spoken to, memorize what you're told, and never color outside the lines unless you're asked to.

We call it "education," but what it really is…is programming.

You really think it's about learning? Then ask yourself why they teach kids to pass tests instead of solve actual problems? Why do they reward regurgitation over innovation? Why do you spend twelve years being measured by your ability to repeat someone else's words, but not once are you asked to explore your own? Because they don't want thinkers! They want workers. People who know how to clock in, follow instructions, and not cause trouble. And they start building those people in the first grade. Hell… maybe even kindergarten.

They train kids to conform before they even know who they are…

Be in class before the bell, sit in rows, follow the rules, stand in line, do your homework, and don't ask why!

Every ounce of natural instinct gets repackaged as "behavioral issues." The wild ones get medicated. The quiet ones get ignored. The bright ones get bored to tears. And the rest of us are just filtered into the middle, where dreams go to die politely, without disturbing anyone.

The Bell doesn't just signal the start of class, though. It signals the end of your freedom. It says: "Your time is not yours anymore. You do what we say, when we say it." And then, eventually, the kids who used to build forts in the woods or draw spaceships on construction paper start asking permission to go to the damn bathroom!

That's not education.

That's domestication.

From the moment you can hold a pencil, they start attaching letters to your work. An "A" means you're smart. A "C" means you're slipping. An "F" means you're a failure. Not just at the work, but as a person. You learn quickly that your worth isn't something you carry inside you. It's something granted or taken away based on how well you perform or follow instructions and repeat information on command. That "grade" isn't just feedback on the task; it's a silent verdict on who you are. And once you've swallowed that whole, you're ready for the adult world, where performance reviews and paychecks keep you chasing the same gold star you've been trained to seek since childhood.

Schools don't teach kids how to find their purpose; they teach them how to meet expectations. It's an assembly line of standardized minds, spit out one after the other with a diploma in one hand and a head full of rules in the other.

And God forbid you question it all!

Challenge the curriculum and you're labeled disruptive. Think too far outside the box and you'll get told to "focus." But focus on what? Worksheets that drain your energy? Outdated textbooks written by people who have no connection to your current generation? Very few teachers are teaching kids how to think for themselves. Most are just teaching them how to obey the script. Though, I do realize there are some who do try, yet even they get steamrolled by the system nine times out of ten.

You ever wonder why school kills imagination? Why a kindergartner is a fountain of ideas, but by the time they graduate high school, they're afraid to even speak their mind? It's because we trained them to believe their worth comes from how well they regurgitate information. What "grade" they get. It's never about how deeply they feel or how uniquely they see the world. We kill so many artists, and so many explorers. We turn them all into "good employees."

And for some reason, we keep calling that "success."

Ugh…

You want to know why society's so full of adults who feel lost, burned out, and disconnected? It's because we never gave them the tools to know who they were in the first place. We taught them how to meet deadlines, not how to discover meaning. We taught them how to chase grades, not how to find themselves.

The education system was never about independence. It was about preparation…

For a life of submission.

And it worked…

We're all the product of that Bell.

So What Now?

Start asking the questions they never let you ask...

What do I love?

What lights me up?

What would I learn if no one told me what mattered?

The system taught you how to follow. Now it's time to unlearn. Read what they never assigned. Build what they never imagined.

The real education begins when you start teaching yourself.

And the first lesson is this: You were never meant to be molded. You were meant to be **uniquely you**!

Chapter 9

The Feed

They say that you're addicted to your phone. That you scroll too much and that you're wasting your life behind a screen.

Yeah, well, maybe that's true...

But this addiction doesn't happen by accident, does it?

You're not weak like so many people love to proclaim. You've been targeted! Your attention, your instincts, and even your self-worth have all been hijacked. All of it was done systematically, deliberately, and with the utmost precision.

These devices you carry in your hands aren't just "neutral tools," they're traps dressed up like conveniences. Every scroll is now calculated. Every swipe is a dopamine hit. Every red notification bubble is a lab-tested trigger designed to spike your curiosity, spark your insecurity, or pull you back in… just in case you were starting to act on your own accord again.

You think you're in control, right? You think you're just browsing through the internet? Well, the truth is, you're being harvested. Your data, your time, your reactions, they're all being sliced up and sold off behind the scenes. You've become the product. And the more predictable your behavior becomes, the more profitable you are to those mining your mind.

The Feed doesn't care what you believe. It doesn't care what's true, either. It only cares what keeps you clicking.

Rage seems to work well these days.

Insecurity works great too. So, that's what it constantly shows you. The content you see is no longer about quality. It's about chemistry. What triggers you? What distracts you? What makes you feel like you're not quite enough?

See, the comparison feature isn't an accident of the system. It **is** the system. You log on to connect, but what you find is a curated illusion. Perfect bodies. Perfect lives. Perfect smiles. Everyone is winning. Everyone is glowing. Everyone seems to have it all figured out… except you. And even when you know it's filtered, and you know it's posed, it still gets under your skin. That's the point. You start adjusting yourself—your opinions, your photos, your personality—to match everything that you see getting rewarded. And you don't even notice that it's happening. Because it's all so subtle.

And then… it becomes *normal.*

That's how it starts: You edit a post to get more likes. You delete one that didn't get enough. You change your tone to avoid judgment. You post a moment of your life not so much to share it, but more-so to perform it. And slowly, your online persona becomes your real one. You don't express things anymore, you *present*. You don't feel emotions, you filter them. You become a brand, a highlight reel, a walking advertisement for a version of yourself that doesn't really exist.

And while you're so busy maintaining that digital mask of yours, your real self—your messy, uncertain, beautiful, *actual self*—starts to fade away. You forget how to be bored, or still, or comfortable without grabbing for a screen to distract you from it all. You forget how to listen to your own thoughts without the background noise. You forget how to speak without worrying how it'll be received. You forget how it is to just *be*.

But let's not pretend this is just about social media. The entire tech ecosystem is built on interruption. You can't even read a damn article without a pop-up, a sidebar ad, a video auto-playing, or a thousand things trying to yank your attention in every which direction! And it works! Because your brain is now trained to crave novelty, to chase stimulation, to avoid depth at all costs. You scroll through 50 videos in 10 minutes and somehow feel exhausted and empty. Why? Simply because you weren't really watching… you were just *distracting*.

And that becomes your baseline.

Eventually, the silence feels unnatural. Rest starts to

feel like you're being lazy. Deep work on yourself feels impossible. You're wired for urgency. But it's a false need. You start mistaking busy for productive, stimulated for satisfied, connected for fulfilled. But you're none of those things, are you? You're just hooked. And the deeper you go, the harder it is to feel any real joy, real presence, real anything! Because everything starts to feel like a shadow of itself. Almost like a simulation.

Even your relationships begin to suffer. You text the people in your own household more than you even talk to them! You send emojis instead of showing real emotions. You check out of real conversations because you're half-listening, half-scrolling, and fully detached from it all.

Worst of all, you know that it's happening. You know The Feed is draining you. You know it's rewiring your brain. But it's easier to keep scrolling than it is to face the discomfort of disconnection. Because the system made damn sure you needed it! Your business is on there. Your social life. Your news. Your validation. Your voice. It's your outlet. Your crutch. So you tell yourself it's not that bad. It's just how the world works now.

You're fine, right?

Deep down, you feel it all. That slow erosion of your true self. That gnawing emptiness in your chest. That strange numbness even when everything "should" be okay.

And you know whats really crazy?

This isn't even about you. It's happening to everyone.

Even me.

Globally. Entire generations being raised to believe that value comes from visibility. That self-worth is measured visually. That if it's not shared online, it didn't happen. That if it didn't go viral, it didn't matter. It's not just attention that's being stolen. It's meaning. And we're paying the price in anxiety, burnout, depression, and disconnection, all while the ones behind the curtain rake in billions of dollars because we're too weak to stop.

But it's not completely your fault. You're a victim, right?

See, the problem is, The Feed doesn't care if you're a victim, if you're lonely, or if you're lost. It doesn't care if your entire sense of self has been fractured and reconstructed around performance. It just wants your eyes open and your finger scrolling.

The second you stop feeding it, it stops feeding you. And that withdrawal you're feeling all of a sudden? That urge to check your phone for no reason? That's not a habit... that's *dependency*.

So what happens when a world that's built on attention addiction finally runs out of attention?

What happens when millions of people wake up and realize they haven't felt present in years?

What happens when we start asking who we were before the algorithm told us who we should be?

Hmm...

So What Now?

Stop letting it run your life.

First, reclaim your attention. That means intentional silence. Daily! Even for just five minutes. Without the phone. Without the noise. Just you and your own damn mind. Let it wander. Let it speak. Let it come alive again! Or, just let it be bored and uncomfortable for a change!

Next, question every impulse you have. When you reach for your phone, why are you reaching for it? Is it boredom? Is it loneliness? Is it avoidance? Don't shame yourself about it. Just notice it.

Awareness is the first break in the chain. Every time you interrupt the automatic scroll, you weaken its hold on you.

Set limits on yourself… not as punishment, but as protection. Turn off notifications. Delete apps that serve as nothing but distractions to you. Move your phone out of reach during meals, during conversations, during moments that matter. Relearn how to be present. Especially for your loved ones. Because they won't be around forever!

And most importantly, reconnect offline. Make space for conversations that don't require "likes." Make room in your day for experiences that don't need to be posted. For presence that isn't filtered or monetized. That's where your real life is happening.

You are **not** your profile. You are **not** your follower count. You are **not** the number of hearts or fire emojis or laughing faces under your last post. You **are** an individual human being. And the more time you spend remembering that, the less power the system has to reduce you to just "content."

Unplugging won't feel natural at first. That's how you know it's necessary. Because the things that heal you often feel like withdrawal before they feel like freedom.

Start there. Stick with it.

And when the silence returns, don't run from it.

Listen.

Because buried beneath all the noise...

You are still in there.

Chapter 10

The Screen

The Screen doesn't just sit in your living room. It sits in your head...

Let me explain...

At first, it was just a box that showed us moving pictures. It was a way to bring a little entertainment into the home. But the box eventually learned your patterns, your desires, and the subtle art of not letting you go, especially after a long day of trading your life for The Paper.

You think you're in control of it because you hold the remote...but really, you're not. The remote is just a leash, and you're the dog being walked.

From the moment you turn it on, it starts pulling you in. With color, sound, and a perfectly measured pace of stimulation. Every cut, every scene change, every laugh track is engineered to keep you from looking away. You're not watching TV; TV is watching you. It's tracking what keeps you in the chair for "just one more episode."

And it's never really "just one more," is it?

The Screen runs in the backdrop of our lives like an open faucet, slowly flooding the mind. We call it "background noise." It fills the silence that you can't tolerate. It fills the boredom you don't know how to replace. It fills the space where your own thoughts might have wandered off to. However, what it ultimately fills you with is emptiness and conditioned thoughts.

Yeah, I said it!

Those news stories you like to binge watch aren't just simply stories, they're delivery systems. Every joke, every update, every dramatic twist has been sifted through layers of approval to make sure the messages align with the ones the system wants in circulation.

Every single frame has been prepared for you.

The screen doesn't just feed you content, it programs the pace at which you live. Sitcoms teach you that problems get solved in a short period of time. Crime shows convince you the bad guys always get caught, and the good guys rarely do anything wrong. News cycles make you believe the world is falling apart faster than it's being built. And commercials tell you exactly how to fill the emptiness they've just stirred up within you.

You think you're relaxing, but you're not.

You're being brainwashed.

And the worst cost in all of this is the price you pay in *time*.

A two-hour movie doesn't just take two hours of your life. It consumes the book you could have read, the project you could have started, the conversation you could have had with someone you care about.

You've been trained to see free time as something to fill, not something to own. The Screen steps in like a loyal but demanding friend, always ready to keep you company, always asking for just one more hour in return. And like any skilled manipulator, it knows how to make you feel like you're the one who chose it.

The truth is, you didn't choose it. The Screen did.

Behind every channel, every streaming service, every "recommended for you" algorithm is a machinery of data collection and behavior shaping. They know how long you'll watch before you need a burst of action. They know which colors keep you calm, which ones keep you alert, and which ones make you hungry enough to order something before the next scene starts.

They even know your bedtime! And they know how to keep you from sticking to it.

The Screen is patient. It doesn't care if you're awake at 2 a.m. or missing your alarm at 6. It doesn't care if you skip meals or even if you skip work! It only cares that you come back. And when you're not in front of it, it follows you… on your phone, your laptop, your tablet, your PC. You don't even have to "turn it on" anymore. It's already there, glowing in your pocket.

But the most dangerous part is that it's not always obvious what it's doing to you.

A single TV show can slip new values into your mind without you ever questioning them, reinforcing biases you may already hold. A commercial can create a need that you didn't know you had. A news program can plant fear deep enough within you to change how you vote, where you shop, and who you trust. And because the screen speaks with the calm authority of familiarity, you don't notice the lies it tells you. Many times, you fall asleep in front of it while it feeds your mind as you doze.

It tells you what's normal. It tells you what's dangerous. It tells you what to want, what to buy, and who to be. And if you don't match the characters you see on it, it tells you you're "less-than."

Am I wrong?

The screen doesn't just rob your free time. Oh, no. It actually rewires the way you think about that time in the first place. It teaches you that silence is awkward, that boredom is a problem, that your own thoughts are too quiet to be worth listening to.

The worst part is the system knows that the earlier it sneaks in, the deeper and faster it can take root. Kids sit in front of it before they can even read, absorbing the tone, pace, and worldviews before they can even form their own. By the time they're old enough to question it, questioning feels wrong, like they're betraying a friend who's always been there for them.

The real tragedy in all this is… we desperately defend it, much like we do the other systems that I've mentioned in this book.

We tell ourselves we "earned" this escape. We call it a reward after a long day. A way to wind down. But no matter how much you dress it up, the trade is always the same: you give it your hours, and it gives you only illusions. And while you're busy inside those illusions, your real life slips quietly past you. The sun sets. The seasons change. Years vanish in the hum of "the background noise."

Some people will say the answer is "balance," but the screen doesn't give a damn about balance. It believes in dominance. It wants the first hour after you wake up and the last before you sleep. It wants to be there when you're sad, when you're bored, when you're lonely, and when you're celebrating. It wants every version of you it can get.

Because the more of you that it owns, the less of you that's left for anything else.

The system knows this. That's why it pours billions into making sure you never truly walk away. Even when you're "done watching," it leaves the light on for you. Flashing there dimly. Urging you to turn it back on. It waits for you. It whispers from the corner of the room; "Are you still watching?"

It knows you'll be back.

The screen doesn't just want your attention. It wants your life.

Just turn it off!

Then notice how much better you feel.

So What Now?

The first step is noticing how often the screen chooses for you.

Count the hours you give to it in a week. Then decide, with intent, how many you're actually willing to hand over to it.

Don't just "watch less." Replace the screen with something that makes you the creator instead of the consumer. Read. Build. Write. Learn a skill. Have conversations that don't involve glowing pixels.

Take back the silence. Sit in it until it stops feeling uncomfortable. That's where your own thoughts live. And the more time you spend there, the harder it is for the system to sell you someone else's thoughts.

The screen will always be there, waiting.

The trick is making sure **you're not**.

Chapter 11

The Role

You were born without a role, remember?

No script to go by, no proverbial costume to wear, no list of lines to say, or rules to follow. But it didn't take long before someone handed you these anyway. Maybe it was your parents, telling you what kind of child you needed to be. Maybe it was school, training you to sit down, shut up, and do what you're told. Maybe it was your first job, teaching you how to smile when you didn't want to, or how to act like you cared about things that didn't matter to you. Somewhere along the way, you got cast in a role, and you learned to play it so well, you forgot that it wasn't really you.

The system thrives on these roles. The "responsible one." The "good employee." The "tough guy." The "loyal friend." Labels are easier to control than people are. If you step outside your role, or your "label," people get uncomfortable. They tell you you're "changing"… as if that's a bad thing. They push you back toward the version of you that they're used to.

Why?

I suppose it's because The Role isn't just for you… it's also for them. It makes *them* feel safe and you more predictable. It tells them where to place you in their mental filing cabinet.

Do you realize that your Role has you adapting just to survive? You start to figure out what gets you praise and what gets you punished, and then you adjust everything accordingly. It's people-pleasing in its purest form. And it's not just because you're weak in this way, but because approval is a currency these days, and you've learned early on that having this currency means safety. So, you become whoever you need to be in the moment. At work, you're the agreeable one. At home, maybe you're the fixer. With friends, you're the "carefree" guy. In public, you're the polite version. Online, you're the highlight reel. And every role that you play takes a little more from the real you until there's less and less of that real you underneath it all.

The danger of this isn't just that you play The Role, it's that The Role starts playing you! You start to believe the mask you're wearing! You convince yourself this is who you've always been. That you chose this life, these traits, these habits you keep. But deep down, there's a part of you that knows better. That little flicker of discomfort you feel when you have to fake a laugh or agree with something that you don't believe. That's the real you, trying to breathe through the suffocating fabric of the part you're playing.

But the system rewards the actors who commit to The Role, so it's tough to break free. Awards go to the ones who never break character. Social circles favor the people who never say anything that rocks the boat. Families brag about the child who follows the expected "grade" path, even if they're miserable doing it. The more convincingly you wear the mask, the more applause you get… and the harder it is to take it off.

But here's the problem: you can't fully live as both the mask and the person underneath. One will always suffocate the other. And if you keep picking the mask— because it's easier, safer, or quieter—eventually you forget how to take the damn thing off! You wake up one day and realize you've spent years doing what you were "supposed" to do without ever stopping to ask why.

Why did you choose this career? Why do you have these beliefs? Why do you keep certain people in your life? Why do you even get out of bed in the morning?

You lose the "why" of you.

And when you lose that, you're easier to manage. People that know who they are don't bend as easily. People that remember why they exist don't give in as quickly. But if the system can keep you chasing applause, approval, and the feeling of being "good," you'll keep playing the part until the curtain falls. Then you'll call it a good life, even if the whole time it was just a well-rehearsed performance.

Honestly, you see it everywhere. You see it in the friend who's terrified of disappointing anyone, so they say "yes" to everything and quietly resent everyone for it. In the coworker who swallows their opinions because "it's not worth the trouble." Or that guy you know who has a heart of gold underneath this rough exterior.

Maybe the scariest part is that we train each other to *stay* in our roles. The moment someone stops playing, we call them selfish, and unreliable. We accuse them of "changing" as if they weren't supposed to.

We don't celebrate people for dropping the act, we shame them for breaking character. Because if they can stop pretending, maybe we can too… and that's scary.

So What Now?

First, you have to admit that The Role exists in you.

That's the hardest step, because The Role is comfortable. It's familiar. It's where you've learned to survive.

But ask yourself this: if nobody was watching, if nobody was judging, if no one was keeping score, how much of what you're doing right now would you still be doing?

That question alone should shake something loose in

you.

Second, start testing small acts of rebellion against your role. Say "no" to something you would normally agree to just to keep the peace. Share an opinion you'd normally keep to yourself. Do something that feels like *you* even if it doesn't fit the script. The goal isn't to rip your life apart overnight. It's to start proving to yourself that the world doesn't collapse when you stop playing the part.

Third, get reacquainted with your "why." What drives you when there's no applause, no paycheck, no pat on the back? If you can't answer that yet… good! That means you've got some digging to do.

Start small. Peel back the layers. Pull traits out of your inner being and look at them closely.

Follow what pulls at you, even if it makes no sense to anyone else. *Especially* if it makes no sense to anyone else!

You were not put here to play a part in someone else's production. You were put here to be a living, breathing, flawed, unpredictable human being with your own thoughts and ideas.

The Role may have kept you safe at one time, but now it's the thing that's keeping you small.

Remove it!

Before you forget what your own damn face looks like!

Chapter 12

The Gavel

The courtroom is designed to resemble a temple for a reason.

The high ceilings, the polished wood all around, the flag, the seal, the raised bench where the judge sits like some all-knowing arbiter of truth. It's all just theater, designed to make you feel small, out of place, and already guilty before you ever even open your mouth.

You're not walking into a house of justice. You're stepping onto a stage.

We call it "the justice system," but let's quit pretending. It's really the "just-us" system.

One set of rules for the rich and powerful, another for everyone else. Those with money can stall, negotiate, or make problems disappear completely. Those without it get processed like cattle, and shoved through a machine that doesn't care who you are as an individual, only that the gears of the system keep turning.

It's certainly not always about "justice!"

Once again, it's just a system of control. The police aren't there to "protect and serve" you, they're there to protect their "masters" and serve the system itself. That's why your neighborhood gets the speed traps while white-collar criminals are at the club playing golf with their buddies. That's why a kid with weed is doing hard time while the pharmaceutical executive who fueled the opioid crisis is cashing in on another bonus check and catching a flight to Bora Bora.

They tell you the system is "blind," but the blindfold has many, many holes in it. It can see your skin color, your bank account, your zip code, and it adjusts itself accordingly. Plea deals, mandatory minimums, bail amounts—these things aren't just random. They're switches that they can flip on or off at will.

Prisons aren't for "rehabilitation" as we've all been led to believe, either. They're just warehouses. Nothing more than human storage units. And they're big business too! Private prisons get paid per head, so the more cells they fill, the more money they make.

Think about that.

There's a profit motive to lock people up. That means the goal isn't *fewer* inmates. It's *more*. And they'll strip you of your freedom and then rent you out as dirt-cheap labor. License plates, call center work, sewing uniforms, and making only pennies per hour. It's modern slavery wrapped in legal slang.

Even when you "serve your time," the system doesn't let you go free. Probation, parole, endless fees, and background checks that keep you from getting decent jobs leave you in a constant state of imprisonment, with only the lingering *illusion* of freedom.

They've built a revolving door, and you're supposed to believe it's an accident. It's not. Recidivism isn't a "failure" of the system, it's the system working as it was intended. They keep the scales tipped just enough to keep certain people cycling in and out of the system for life. I've seen it happen to people I've known.

And here's the dirtiest secret of all: it needs you to be scared. Not just of breaking the law, but of crossing it, questioning it, or stepping out of line. They don't care if you're innocent or guilty. They only care that you know that they can ruin you in an instant. That's why they can raid the wrong house, shoot the wrong man or woman, and still walk away untouched. The message is clear: "we hold the hammer, and we decide where it falls."

It's all arrogance!

Watch any high-profile case involving the elite, and you'll see it. Charges dropped, deals made behind closed doors, "technicalities" that magically appear when the defendant is rich enough to afford a defense team that bills more per hour than you make in a month. Meanwhile, public defenders are juggling a hundred cases at once, trying to keep up with a conveyor belt of human lives moving too fast to save.

Once again, this damn system isn't broken! This is not even a flaw. This is the design!

A real justice system would close loopholes, shrink prison populations, focus on truth over conviction rates, rehabilitate those who would accept it. But the system we have currently feeds on convictions, fines, and asset seizures. It doesn't just punish… it profits! And it doesn't just stop with the courts or the cops. It's the entire web around them. Lawmakers writing "tough on crime" bills to get re-elected, police unions shielding officers from accountability, corporations building surveillance tech and selling it to local departments, private prison lobbies pushing for harsher sentencing.

Every player in the game gets paid as long as the game keeps going.

Meanwhile, you're told to just trust it, respect it, believe it's the great equalizer. And if you don't? They'll make an example of you.

The Gavel sends messages. Messages like: stay in your lane, don't fight back, don't question why a system that's supposed to serve you is stacked against you from the start.

So What Now?

Stop pretending it's something it's not. Start by knowing the rules better than they want you to. Learn about your rights and the loopholes they use to circumvent them. Stop swallowing every headline about "justice served" without looking at who benefited. Support bail reform, sentencing reform, jury nullification, and any initiative that strips profit out of incarceration.

Most of all, stop living like you're powerless. The system counts on your silence and your ignorance. Talk about it, call it what it is, refuse to glorify it! Because every hammer that drops starts with someone in power deciding where to swing it, and the only way to stop being under it is to start pushing back.

The Gavel's not there to protect you. It's there to remind you who's in charge. Until you see that, you're just another defendant waiting for your turn to be played.

Chapter 13

The Battlefield

You hear it all the time: "our soldiers are fighting for your freedom." They tell you it's about country, honor, service, and sacrifice. They wrap it all in flags, parades, and speeches that sound like they came from an ancient text. But strip away the music and the medals, and what you've really got is one of the biggest, bloodiest businesses on the planet.

And business is booming! (Pun intended.)

The "Battlefield" isn't just overseas. It's right here, in our classrooms, in our movies, in our video games, and in the way kids are groomed to see war as noble before they can even see it as deadly.

You know how early it starts? Walk into any high school cafeteria when the recruiters are set up with their fresh haircuts, shiny smiles, free pens and keychains with the branch's logo on them. They act like they're offering an opportunity. College money, travel, a way out of your boring small town. But they don't talk about the PTSD. They don't mention anything about watching your friends get blown apart, or the trauma that comes later from knowing you took one or more lives of people they told you were your "enemies." They don't talk about coming home to a system that forgets you the moment your usefulness runs out. They frame it as "service," but what they're really selling is an illusion.

They want to make sure to sign you up before you're old enough to legally buy a beer. For the sole reason that young and impressionable minds are easier to mold and manipulate.

They prey on uncertainty. On kids who feel stuck. Families who can't afford college. Teenagers looking for purpose. They know exactly what they're doing because they've been doing it for decades. My own twins got swept into it, and I saw firsthand how slick the pitch is. All the pride and promise on the front end, then all the silence on the back end after you're broken.

It's not a coincidence. It's a damn sales funnel! And the product is human bodies to feed the machine.

Make no mistake; this isn't about protecting you. It's about protecting interests. Corporate, political, strategic. Wars aren't fought to end conflict anymore. They're fought to sustain it. Every bomb dropped, every bullet fired, every contract signed for tanks, drones, and gear is a payday for someone. The military-industrial complex isn't just a unit… it's an economy.

And peace?

That's bad for business.

Look at the defense budget. Trillions of dollars poured into weapons manufacturing while our societies crumble, our healthcare rots, and entire cities go without clean water. Look at how the same contractors win the same contracts year after year, charging billions for projects that run over budget and under deliver. And nobody cares, because the profit's guaranteed. Look at how many retired generals slide right into cushy corporate jobs for the very companies that sold the weapons they ordered.

It's a revolving door lined with gold.

And here's the part that nobody wants to admit: the military doesn't just fight wars, it creates them. Regime change, proxy wars, "training exercises" that mysteriously escalate into full-blown conflicts, all of it under the banner of "defense." We're told it's about "spreading democracy," but somehow it always seems to line up with resource-rich regions, strategic territory, or areas where corporate interests stand to gain something.

Wars don't just *happen*. They're *chosen*. And someone always gets paid. BIG.

Meanwhile, the soldiers, the ones who believed the sales pitch, are the expendable part of the deal. They're paraded around when it's time to rally public support, and then left in the shadows when they come back broken.

Suicide rates among veterans are through the roof!

Access to health/mental care is a bureaucratic nightmare, and the people who pushed them into the uniform are nowhere to be found. The recruiter who swore they'd "always have your back" won't answer your calls now. And the politicians who voted for the war will never remember you even existed.

And yet the cycle keeps going because the propaganda machine is relentless. War is always packaged as heroism. Service is sold as the highest form of citizenship and patriotism. Movies, games, and commercials keep the image clean and shiny so the next generation doesn't see the blood and the body bags. And by the time they're old enough to question it, the papers are signed and they're on the bus to boot camp.

It's honestly a perfect business model. Perpetual war means perpetual profit. Endless recruitment means an endless supply of fresh bodies. And a population trained to salute and thank you for your service without ever asking what that service was for is the final piece… the cultural shield that keeps the machine running without any resistance what-so-ever.

So What Now?

Stop letting recruiters waltz into schools unchallenged. Talk to kids before the military does. Show them the full picture, not the polished one. If you're a parent, have the uncomfortable conversations early. Don't wait for the uniform to walk into the cafeteria with a clipboard.

Push for transparency. Where are the defense dollars going? Who's profiting from the wars we fight? Why are the same companies writing the same contracts year after year? Follow the money, and you'll find the motive.

And most of all, stop swallowing the idea that war is inevitable. It's not! It's engineered! And as long as we keep feeding the machine with our sons, daughters, brothers, and sisters, it will never stop turning.

The Battlefield isn't just "over there." It's in your schools, in your living room, and if you're not paying attention, it's already at your front door!

And while we're on the subject, can we finally kill the tired lie that we're "fighting for freedom"? What kind of stupid do they think we are? Fighting for *our* freedom in a country most of us couldn't find on a map?

Or wait… are we killing them for *their* freedom?

Hmm…

Because, sure, nothing says liberty like foreign boots on your soil and drones overhead.

They wrap it in red, white, and blue, but underneath it's always the same colors:

Blood red and profit green.

Chapter 14

The Watchers

You're being watched.

Right now, as you read this.

Not in a paranoid "tin foil hat" kind of way, but in a very real, very measurable way.

Your phone knows where you slept last night, when you woke up, and how many steps you've taken today. Your car remembers where you've driven. Your credit card logs every purchase you make. Your streaming service tracks what you watch, when you pause, and how often you rewind. Even the "private" mode on your browser is a joke. The only thing it hides is your history from the person who uses your PC/laptop after you.

The system still sees it.

The surveillance state has been here for a while. Cameras sit on street corners, license plate readers track your car, doorbell cameras that your neighbors installed for "security" feeds footage into police databases. Microphones in your smart devices "activate" when you say the magic word (whatever word that may be).

Everything you touch, click, or speak is collected, stored, and run through algorithms you'll never see.

It's not just the government that's watching you, though. Corporations are on the front line of the modern spy game. They call it "data," but what they really mean is *you*. Your habits, preferences, and weak spots are all collected. They'll scrape it from your apps, social media, shopping sites, and even your loyalty cards. They build a profile so detailed it can predict what you'll want before you even think about it. Then they sell that profile to advertisers, political campaigns, intelligence agencies, and even your insurance companies.

If you think that you're safe because you're "not doing anything wrong," you're very naive. The Watchers don't care about right or wrong. They care about control, patterns, and probabilities. "Predictive policing" is already here. Software is being tested as I write this that decides who is "likely" to commit a crime based on where you live, who you talk to, and what you post. If the algorithm says you're a risk, you could find yourself on a list without ever knowing or even breaking any laws.

Crazy, huh?

The real insanity of all this, like many other systems I've already mentioned, is that you're helping build the system yourself. You pay for the devices, you install the cameras, you download the apps without reading the permissions, you wear the fitness tracker that sends your heart rate to a server in another country.

They don't have to bug your home by force.

You've invited them in!

Even when you think you've avoided it, you haven't. You use cash instead of a card? There's a camera at the register. You leave your phone at home? Your friend's phone will log your location when you meet up (look it up). You deleted an app? Too late. The data's already been sold and copied. This isn't about one leak or one hack, it's a net so tight that even if you swim like hell, you're still drowning in it.

Watching is only the beginning, though. The next step is steering. If they can see/hear everything you do, they can also shape it. Targeted ads aren't just about selling products. They're about selling narratives, candidates, and lifestyles. Every headline you read, every trending topic in your feed, and every video that "just so happens" to pop up is tailored to keep you inside a belief bubble that was built specifically for you.

The worst part is that it works. Most people don't notice the fence until it's already around them. They think they're making free choices, when in reality the system has been nudging them towards those choices the entire time. And it's all done with a constant, quiet influence that's so subtle you mistake it for your own ideas.

We've gone from "Big Brother" to millions of little brothers in our pockets, on our walls, and in our hands.

The Watchers no longer have to hide. They can put cameras in plain sight and people will thank them for the "safety."

It's become completely absurd!

So What Now?

Stop pretending you're invisible. You're not. Know what's being collected and by who. Read the permissions. Audit your devices. Remove what you don't need. Limit what you give away freely, because every scrap of information will be used. If not today, then certainly tomorrow.

Understand that privacy is not about hiding. It's about control. The less they know, the less they can predict, manipulate, or preemptively punish you for. Use encrypted messaging. Ditch loyalty programs. Turn off "always listening" features. Not because you're a criminal, but because you're not a fool.

Spread awareness. The watchers depend on compliance and apathy. If you accept constant surveillance as "just the way things are," you've already surrendered. Push back. Talk about it. Teach your kids the value of privacy before it disappears entirely.

Once they can see everything, they don't need permission to act. And by the time you realize the bars are closing in, it won't matter how loud you scream.

The Watchers won't miss a thing.

Chapter 15

The Overlords

They sell you the illusion of choice.

Different logos. Different packaging. Different commercials with actors pretending to be versions of you and your family. But look hard enough at it all and you find out that the same handful of companies own almost everything on the shelves. Your "options" are just different faces of the same beast… and that beast is laughing all the way to the bank.

Corporations don't just sell you products. They're writing the rules of the entire system. They bankroll politicians, draft legislation, and lobby for loopholes big enough to drive their armored trucks of profits through. And while you're arguing over the left wing or the right wing, they're busy buying both sides, so that no matter who comes out on top, their interests win along with them.

They have more influence than most governments do! Some of them have more money than entire countries! They can move jobs across borders overnight, crash local economies, and then sweep in to buy the remnants at a huge discount. They can squeeze suppliers until they break, and then swallow them whole. And they do it all while smiling at you through billion-dollar PR campaigns about "community" and "family values."

These Overlords have one religion:

Growth.

The growth is not for you, though. It's not even for society, but growth for their bottom line. If something doesn't feed the shareholders, it dies. Worker safety, product quality, and environmental responsibility all comes in second place to quarterly earnings. If cutting corners saves a penny, they'll do it in a heartbeat, and if someone gets hurt in the process, they'll just settle out of court quietly and keep on moving.

They own the media that you consume daily. They own the platforms where you complain about them.

Think about that.

They own the supply chains that bring you your food, your clothes, your medicine. They own patents on seeds, on life-saving drugs, on the technology you use every single day. And if you think that competition will save you, think again! The moment a small company starts making noise, The Overlords either buy it, bury it, or bleed it out until it completely disappears.

You know that phone in your pocket? It was built to break. That appliance that you just bought for your spouse? It was designed to fail right after the warranty runs out. It's called 'planned obsolescence,' and it keeps you spending over and over again. They don't want you to buy something once and be done. Nooo! They want you in a cycle; always upgrading, always replacing, always paying.

They also want you loyal to them, which is why they play the "brand identity" game. You're not just buying shoes, you're joining a "movement." You're not just drinking coffee, you're part of a "community." They wrap products in identity so tightly that criticizing them feels like it's an attack on *you*. They want you defending the hand that's picking your pocket.

Tricky, huh?

But don't kid yourself for one minute…

They know you better than you know yourself. Every purchase, every click, every location ping gets fed into their data vaults. They know your habits, your cravings, and your weaknesses. They know when you're most likely to splurge and what image will tip you over the edge. They use that knowledge to steer you where they want you to go, while convincing you that it was your idea all along.

Governments talk about regulating them, but The Overlords are often the ones writing the regulations. They set the bar low enough to step over and high enough to crush any smaller competitor. Fines are meaningless when you make more in a day than you lose in court. They can break laws, get caught, pay a penalty, and keep doing it over and over because the math still works in their favor at the end of the day.

They survive by staying untouchable. If a factory disaster happens in another country, they blame the contractor. If toxic chemicals show up in your food, they point to "supply chain issues." They have layers of buffers between them and accountability, so no matter how bad the damage is, their hands always stay clean in the public eye.

And while all this is happening, they market themselves as heroes. They sponsor charity runs. They donate just enough money to make headlines. They release "sustainability reports" full of buzzwords and empty promises. It's all image management, designed to make you forget they're the same demons causing the problems they claim to be solving.

As I've said before, we don't live in a democracy. We live in a corporate oligarchy that's wearing a democratic mask. The Overlords don't need to control every politician, law, or agency. They just need to control enough of them to keep the gears turning.

So, as long as you keep playing their game, they'll keep winning it.

So What Now?

First, stop pretending you're powerless.

Choose where your money goes. Every dollar is a meaningful vote, and they're counting on yours. Support small, local businesses whenever possible. Buy less, buy better, and keep what you own for as long as you can. Break their damn cycle of obsolescence!

Second, pay attention to the mergers, the buyouts, the quiet deaths of once-independent companies. When your "choices" start looking the same, they probably are.

Learn who owns what. Follow the supply chains. When you know the connections, you start seeing the web for what it is.

Finally, speak the truth about what they are. Don't let the glossy ads and sponsored posts convince you that they're benevolent giants. Call out their exploitation, challenge their narratives, teach your kids that a brand is not an identity.

The Overlords won't give up control willingly. They've built their empires on your loyalty, your distraction, and your dependence.

Stop giving it to them!

Chapter 16

The Script

There is definitely a Script, in case I haven't already made you aware of it…

It's not written on paper somewhere, and it's not kept in some secret vault. It exists in the headlines, sound bites, and in the way every major news outlet seems to say the same thing at the same time. You can change the channel or scroll through different news feeds, but the tone and structure will remain the same. The same stories appear in the same order, framed with the same angles, dressed in slightly different colors to match the audience they're trying to hold.

None of this is by coincidence, it's all a planned choreography.

The news you watch is supposed to inform you. That's the premise most of us grew up believing in, right? It's the reason we're told to "stay tuned" or to "keep up with current events." But in reality, the modern news machine doesn't exist to keep you informed at all. It's simply there to keep you aligned with a chosen narrative, with a set of acceptable opinions, and a world view that benefits the same systems that are pulling the strings behind the scenes.

Every day begins with a decision about what will be covered and what will be ignored. This decision isn't randomly generated because it reflects priorities that go far beyond public interest. Stories that threaten the stability of those in power are either softened until they lose their edge or they're buried under layers of other noise until they disappear entirely. Meanwhile, stories that reinforce the preferred narrative are amplified until they drown out everything else.

This is where the idea of "The Script" comes in. The Script is the invisible set of instructions that ensures consistency across the entire media landscape. It determines which facts are repeated and which are left out.

It dictates the entire emotional framework.

Is the story meant to scare you? Should it make you angry? Maybe it should make you feel hopeless? The Script decides it all. Even the language they use is engineered. Certain words are repeated over and over again because repetition makes them feel true, even when they're not. (Think "Weapons of Mass Destruction")

Once you start noticing it, you'll hear the same phrases

on different networks. You'll see the same headlines written in different fonts. The talking heads will change, but the message stays exactly same.

When one story fizzles out, a new one comes to life to replace it.

Suddenly, every outlet is covering the same new crisis or scandal, and yesterday's "urgent" story fades away like it never happened. This constant rotation keeps the public in a state of mild anxiety, always waiting for the next big thing to drop, always reliant on the same sources to tell them what matters most.

The Script doesn't work by force, it works by trust. People don't think of themselves as following a script. They think they're making their own conclusions based on what they see and hear. But if all the information you're given comes from the same approved menu, your "conclusion" was already chosen for you before you even started thinking about it! The illusion of choice keeps people from noticing the limits placed around their understanding.

One of the most effective tools in The Script is "selective context." Facts are rarely outright fabricated, because outright lies can be exposed. Instead, the facts are shaped and placed into a frame that tells you how to interpret them. They're manipulated. It's like looking at a photograph that's been cropped so tightly that you have no idea what was just outside the edge. You believe you're seeing the whole picture, but the rest of the truth has been cut away. This is how the same event can be reported in completely different ways, both technically true, yet leading the viewer to completely opposite conclusions.

The Script also thrives on emotional triggers. The more emotionally charged a story is, the less likely you are to question it. Outrage, fear, and moral superiority are powerful drugs, and the news outlets know how to deliver them. A steady diet of these emotions keeps people in a reactive state, unable to slow down long enough to examine the story itself. This is why The Script often turns complex issues into simple good-versus-evil battles. Nuance is the enemy of control. The more you see the "other side" as dangerous or ignorant, the less likely you are to question your own side.

The repetition of The Script across different outlets creates something else: social proof. If you hear the same message from multiple sources, you're more likely to believe it's accurate. Remember earlier how we talked about corporations owning the whole gambit of companies? This is why the system cannot tolerate large-scale dissent within mainstream channels.

One rogue voice with a large enough audience can disrupt the illusion of agreement, which is why dissenting journalists are often silenced, discredited, or pushed to the fringes. When that happens, the audience is told that those voices are "unreliable" or "dangerous," which conveniently protects The Script from being challenged.

People often underestimate how much of their worldview is shaped by this constant stream. It's not just about politics or world events. The Script influences what people value, what they fear, who they trust, and even how they define right and wrong. It's the background noise of modern life, and like any constant sound, it becomes invisible over time. You stop noticing it, but it keeps shaping you anyway.

The internet was supposed to break The Script. At first, it seemed like it might just do that. Anyone could publish their own perspective, an audiences could find information outside the traditional channels. But as the internet grew, the system learned to adapt. The same forces that controlled television and print began controlling online visibility. Search engines and social platforms now determine what rises to the top and what disappears into the void. Once again, the audience believes they're seeing a broad range of information, but the real choices have already been made for them.

The most dangerous part of The Script is that it teaches you what and how to think without ever admitting that it's doing this. It sets the boundaries of acceptable thought, and as long as you stay within those boundaries, you feel informed, and engaged. You feel like a good citizen. But step outside those boundaries, and you're labeled as misinformed, extreme, or even unwell. This is how the system remains self-sustaining. It doesn't need to silence every dissenting voice. It only needs to convince the majority to ignore them. So, pay attention!

Breaking free from The Script isn't easy. It requires a conscious decision to seek out information from sources that don't agree with each other. It requires questioning not only the story itself but the structure of the story. And then resisting the emotional bait that tries to hook you before you have a chance to think.

If you can see The Script for what it is, you can begin to read between the lines. You can notice what's not being said. You can recognize when your emotions are being played with. You can hear the "rhythm" of the narrative and know when it's shifting to guide you somewhere you didn't choose to go.

Awareness doesn't make you immune to influence, but it gives you the power to step back and decide whether to play along or not.

The system counts on you never doing that. It counts on you mistaking the menu for the meal. The Script won't disappear because you stop believing it, but it will lose its hold over you. And when enough people step outside its framework, the story finally changes.

So What Now?

Stop taking the news at face value. Watch and listen to less of it, and when you do, watch it like an investigator, not a believer. Ask yourself who benefits from you seeing this story in this way. Pay attention to what's missing just as much as what's shown.

Start diversifying your sources. Read from outlets that don't agree with each other, and not just the ones the system approves. Look for independent journalists, long-form interviews, raw footage, and unedited statements. The less filtered the information, the less scripted your understanding will be.

Resist the emotional bait.

When a headline makes you instantly furious or afraid, pause for a few minutes. That's exactly the reaction the system wants from you, because it keeps you from thinking. Sit with the feelings for a bit, then ask yourself if the facts still hold up once the heat of the emotion cools down.

Talk to people outside your bubble. See how the same story looks from a different angle. You may not agree with them, but you'll start to see how much of your own thinking has been shaped by repetition and framing.

Chapter 17

The Cure

They call it "healthcare," but it's not even remotely about your health anymore.

It's all about revenue.

It's about keeping you just well enough to keep paying them, and just sick enough to keep coming back to pay them even more. The "healthcare" system doesn't make its money when you're healthy. It makes its money when you're hooked on prescriptions, and appointments, and hooked on treatments that manage symptoms but never touch on the root cause of your illness.

Pharmaceutical companies don't exist to cure disease. Because if they cured it, the cash flow would completely stop. A one-time cure is a one-time payment. But a lifetime of medication is a subscription plan, and they've turned our illnesses into the most lucrative subscription service on Earth. You're not a patient anymore, you're an account number with a recurring payment plan.

Look at how many "conditions" suddenly exploded into public awareness once there was a new drug to sell. We have restless leg syndrome, seasonal depression, "mild" anxiety, and allegedly ADHD in record numbers. Are any of these conditions even real? For some people, I imagine they are, but it's odd to me how so many now are diagnosed with these and how they all started appearing out of nowhere at the turn of the millennium when the drug companies started realizing that their plan was working.

See, Big Pharma's got the medical establishment in their pockets. Doctors are often trained to treat symptoms, not causes, because causes can be messy. Causes can mean lifestyle changes, diet changes, stress reduction. These are things that can't be patented. But a pill can be patented. A procedure can be billed. And when the pharmaceutical rep takes the doctor and his staff out to lunch and hands them free samples, bonuses, and a slick pitch to back it all up, it's easy for that doctor to "recommend" that brand-name drug instead of exploring other solutions.

Insurance companies are part of the scam as well. They decide what treatments you can and can't get, and all based on what's profitable for them. They'll deny a life-saving procedure on a technicality while approving an endless supply of maintenance drugs. Why? Because the procedure is a one-time cost. The drugs keep you in the system indefinitely.

And don't even think that we're only talking about physical health. Mental health has become another goldmine for them. Are you feeling down? There's a pill for that. Trouble in the bedroom? There's a pill for that. Can't sleep? There's a pill for that too. Never mind that many of these drugs come with side effects that require even more drugs to manage. It's a cascade of bullshit, and every step down the line is another invoice on your desk!

The marketing is also relentless…

You see it every night on TV… smiling actors, soft music, promises of a better life if you just "ask your doctor." They sell you hope in 30-second segments, with the side effects sped up at the end so you barely register that the "cure" can cause strokes, suicidal thoughts, organ damage, or even death. And yet people line up for this shit, because the alternative — actually changing how they live — is harder, slower, and not heavily advertised.

Meanwhile, the prices are outrageous! Drugs that cost a few dollars to make are sold for hundreds, even thousands! People in other countries buy the same medication for a fraction of the cost, but here in the good 'ole U S of A., you're told that's just "how the system works." And if you can't afford it? Too bad. Pay up, go without, or die quietly.

That's the choice you get to make.

The ugly truth is that sickness is profitable, and prevention simply isn't. Clean food, clean water, reduced pollution, stress-free living; these would save more lives than any pill ever could. But those things don't generate quarterly earnings. So we get processed junk food, polluted cities, high-stress jobs, and a medical system designed to mop up the damage for a fee.

They've trained you to think that healthcare is a safety net. But it's not. It's a business plan. And in this business plan, the healthiest outcome for them is you staying alive, but never actually getting better.

So What Now?

First, stop waiting for the system to save you. It's not built for that. Take ownership of what you can control… like what you eat, how active you are, how you manage your stress. The more you take care of yourself, the less leverage they have over you.

Second, question every prescription. Ask what exactly it's suppose to be treating. Ask what caused the problem in the first place. Ask if there's another way. If your doctor can't answer these questions or gets defensive, that there is your red flag. Move on!

Third, push for transparency and affordability. Demand disclosure on who's funding medical research and who stands to profit from it. And when possible, support alternative and preventive care that isn't tied to

Big Pharma's leash.

Most of all, remember this: **you're not their priority.**

Their priority is their shareholders. The moment you accept that, you stop being a willing participant in their experiment. Because the real cure isn't in their pill bottles.

The real cure is breaking free from the belief that they actually want to see you well.

Chapter 18

The Safety Net

They sold you the dream of security and then made it a law. They told you that as long as you kept paying for your insurance, you'd be safe. They said that no matter what came your way, whether it was the accident, the fire, the illness, or the storm, they'd be there to help you. But the truth is this: they built The Safety Net to hold your money, not you or your belongings.

It was never designed to protect you or your things. It was designed to keep you trapped, paying into a promise that they never planned to keep.

Ever notice how they play on your fear? Every commercial, every promise they make, every smiling agent looking you in the eye and telling you that they care about you. They have you imagining the wreck on the highway, the hospital bill, the house fire, the flood, the "what if's" that you can't stop thinking about. They make you afraid, then they sell you The Safety Net. But it's not relief they're offering you…

It's dependency.

Month after month, you pay for peace of mind. You think you're paying for security, but what you're really doing is feeding a machine that profits when you don't use it and fights you when you do. The second you *really* need your insurance, you find out how little you were actually buying.

You've seen this happen to friends and family, or maybe you know it firsthand for yourself. You or someone you know pays for the policy for years, believing they're covered. Then disaster hits and suddenly the policy "doesn't apply." There's always a reason too. Always some "loophole." Always a technicality buried in fine print written by people whose only job is to protect the corporation from paying you what they promised.

Health insurance is probably the worst offender out there. You can spend thousands every year on premiums, copays, and deductibles, and when something serious happens to you, you still end up drowning in medical debt. Hospitals and insurers fight each other over what's "approved," but you're the one that gets stuck with all the bills. People lose their homes while being fully insured. Families go bankrupt while "covered." And none of it's by accident.

That's the system working exactly as it was designed.

But it doesn't stop with health insurance. Life, auto, home, disaster, it's all the same game in a different suit. Pay us now, they say, so you don't lose everything later. But when later comes, you learn the rules were never written for you. A storm tears off your roof, but the damage is classified as "flood-related" instead of "wind-related." Denied. A car accident puts you out of work, but your policy doesn't cover lost wages. Denied. Your house catches fire, but replacement cost doesn't mean what you thought it meant. Denied again.

They don't care what happens to you or your belongings. They care about the math. The entire business model depends on one thing: collecting as much as possible while paying out as little as possible.

And now it's getting worse.

The next layer of robbery is already here. Algorithms are making decisions about your life before you even know you're on the list. Your driving habits, your grocery purchases, your gym attendance, your online searches, your medical history—it's all being tracked, measured, and scored by systems you'll never even see. The discount they dangle for installing a tracking app in your car isn't a perk. It's surveillance. The smartwatch on your wrist, the phone in your pocket, they're all feeding data into profiles that decide how much you pay, if you qualify at all, and how fast they'll deny you when disaster strikes.

And the worst part is; we've been conditioned to accept it all. We joke about insurance companies being crooks, or how it's "all a racket," but we keep paying them anyway, don't we? We shrug when our premiums go up and coverage shrinks. We tell ourselves, "That's just how it works." But it's not. That's just how *they've* built it to work!

The truth is simple. The Safety Net they sold you was never meant to catch you. It was meant to hold you in place, keep you compliant, and keep you paying until the day you finally need them... the day when they let you fall anyway.

So what now?

Stop pretending the system was designed for your benefit. Stop waiting for their version of security and start building your own. That doesn't mean living without protection. It means taking control of where your protection comes from. Build smaller, human safety nets. Local ones, from people you trust. Shared funds with friends and family. Community groups that actually help each other instead of making you prove you're "eligible" while you're bleeding on the floor. Learn the basics of self-reliance, because every skill you gain is one less piece of leverage they hold over you.

The truth is, the people around you will save you long before a corporation ever will. Once you realize the game, you can step out of it. You can start weaving your own safety net. One that they can't rip apart when you need it most.

Chapter 19

The Table

The food on your table isn't just food, it's a creation by a system that doesn't care if you live well, but only if you keep buying its products.

I mean, think about it, "organic" used to mean grown in healthy soil, free from chemicals and manipulation. Now it's just a sticker they slap on produce shipped thousands of miles, sprayed with "approved" pesticides, and wrapped in plastic. It's all just marketing dressed up as morality… and most people swallow it whole without ever tasting the lie.

Every day, grocery stores throw away mountains of perfectly edible food. Locked dumpsters behind chains and padlocks, guarded like treasure. They're not keeping it from pests, but from people. Us! They'd rather bleach the bread and trash the vegetables than risk a lawsuit from someone eating "outdated" foods. Meanwhile, children go to bed hungry in the same city where this food rots under fluorescent lights and corporate policy.

Expiration dates are not a science; they're a sales tactic! Nothing more than a little ink printed on a package that controls your behavior. You believe it only because they told you to. Perfectly good milk poured down drains, fruit tossed because of a simple bruise, meat destroyed not because it's spoiled, but because the clock ran out on its barcode. This is the logic of a system that measures value in profit margins, and not in human needs.

Even "fresh" is an illusion at this point. That apple you bought might have been picked a year ago, stored in a cold warehouse to slow its decay. The lettuce in your fridge was probably washed in chlorine water to keep it "crisp" until it's bagged in plastic and sold for triple the cost of growing it. And every single bite is tracked, from farm to fork, to maximize corporate efficiency, instead of your health.

You don't see whats behind it all; the soil stripped bare by monoculture farming, the bees dying off from toxic pesticides, the migrant workers paid next to nothing to harvest the crops. You don't see the small farmers crushed under the weight of contracts that force them into debt and dependence on mega-corporations for seed, feed, and chemicals. You just see shelves full of "choices" that all lead back to the same handful of companies we discussed earlier. We are so far removed from the source of our food that most people couldn't grow a tomato plant to save their life!

And that's just sad!

But the cruelty runs deeper than just hunger. It's in the engineered addiction we have to sugar, salt, and fat, the calculated design of food to hit your brain like a drug. It's in the manipulation of "low-fat" and "healthy" labels while pumping products full of chemicals your body can't even process.

And while you eat, the machine just keeps on turning. The farmers who grow the real food get pushed out. The corporations that control much of the food system patent life itself through genetically modified seeds. Governments subsidize corn syrup while fresh produce prices climb. And you're told this is the only way to "feed the world," as if starvation is a supply problem instead of a greed problem!

So What Now?

Grow something.

Anything.

Even if it's a single tomato plant on your porch.

Learn where your food comes from and what real food tastes like. Buy from local farmers when you can. Support co-ops and community gardens. Stop falling for the labels, and the "sell-by" dates.

And when you see waste, speak up! Because silence keeps the dumpster locked.

The Table doesn't have to be set by them. Build and set your own! While you still have choices.

Chapter 20

The Forgotten

We don't like to talk about getting old, do we?

The silence about this subject is so loud.

We've basically built a culture that worships youth, productivity, and speed, while quietly shoving the people who can no longer keep up in our society into the background.

They're out of sight, out of mind, and out of the way.

You spend your entire life contributing to society. You work, you pay taxes, you raise families, and you build communities, believing that when your body starts to slow down there will be dignity on the other side. You expect that the system you supported for all those decades will take care of you when you need it the most.

But for millions of people, that promise is a blatant lie. The reality is brutal!

Once you're no longer "useful," the system doesn't know what to do with you. The elderly are simply made invisible. And worse than invisible, they become profitable. Nursing homes, assisted living facilities, and elder care services are sold as sanctuaries, but too many of them are built on squeezing every last drop of value from people who can no longer afford to fight back.

If you've ever walked the quiet hallways of a nursing home, you know what I'm talking about. My mother was a nurses aid in one for years, so I saw firsthand. The blank stares. The silence that's broken only by the distant sound of TVs that were left on for what little "company" they provide. Understaffed and underpaid workers rushing between too many patients to give anyone any real attention. Corners are cut because time is money. And in these places, money always wins. And neglect is *way too easy* in here!

It's not just the disregard of our parents and grandparents, though. It's the overmedication, the billing fraud, and the "warehousing" of human beings while claiming to provide care, and stacking profits on the backs of people who have no strength left to resist.

Families struggle under these impossible choices. Most people can't afford twenty-four-hour in-home care. They can't possibly leave their jobs, and they certainly can't pay out of pocket for private solutions. So they do what the system expects them to do. They hand their loved ones over to institutions, hoping they'll be safe.

Sometimes they are.

But all too often… they're not.

Meanwhile, pharmaceutical companies see the elderly as walking goldmines. More prescriptions, more treatments, more insurance claims, more revenue. Instead of focusing on quality of life, the focus shifts to "managing" symptoms indefinitely. If you live long enough, you become a spreadsheet line item. Another account to be billed and another resource to be drained.

We're not just failing elderly individuals. We're failing entire generations! We're also failing ourselves. Because one day, if we're (un)lucky enough to live that long, we'll be next in line. And if we keep ignoring what's happening, nothing will change by the time we get there. It may even get worse than it is now!

The deeper truth is just as uncomfortable. The elderly care crisis isn't an accident. It's a symptom of how our systems decide who matters. It tells us that if you're producing, you're valuable. If you're consuming, you're tolerable. But if you become dependent, you're pushed aside and forgotten about. That's the cold truth of an economy that measures human worth in productivity and profit.

And the problem with this system is only getting worse. People are living longer than ever before, but we're not preparing for it. Entire industries exist to "manage" aging populations while avoiding the harder question...

Why do we treat people like problems once they stop

working for us?

Technology could change everything, but right now it's being used to cut costs, not improve lives. AI-powered monitoring tools are replacing human caregivers, instead of supporting them. Data algorithms decide what care someone "deserves" based on profitability, not need. Every advancement that could make things better ends up in the hands of companies chasing quarterly earnings instead of human dignity.

The biggest lie that we're sold is that we'll all have someone to care for us when the time comes. But fewer families live together now. Fewer children can afford to take time off work to support aging parents. We've outsourced the responsibility of caring for the people who cared for us. And the system we've handed them over to isn't built on compassion… it's built on efficiency and profit.

We need to stop pretending this is just "how it is." Because it's not! It is how we've allowed it to become!

So what now?

We start by looking directly at what we've been conditioned to ignore. We have to see the people in those quiet halls, those underfunded facilities, those homes where someone is just trying to make it through the day without help. We have to stop treating aging as an individual failure and start treating it as a collective responsibility. These people are the wise ones among us, they're the ones who raised us, watched over us, cared for us, and we're just throwing them away like trash!

It's disgusting!

We need to build support systems outside the ones designed to exploit them.

It means families, neighbors, and communities pooling resources. It means creating shared spaces where elders are not hidden away but integrated, respected, and heard. It means questioning policies, demanding oversight, and refusing to let neglect hide behind closed doors.

Because dignity isn't something you earn. It's not tied to what you produce, how much you make, or how useful you are to someone else's bottom line. Dignity belongs to all of us, from the first day we're born until the last breath we take.

We forgot that somewhere along the way.

It's time that we remember.

Chapter 21

The Green Mask

They tell you that The Green Mask is there to protect the planet. That it was created to shield the Earth from the damage we've been causing it. To heal the air, the water, the soil. And the way they say it, you'd think the people behind it are the heroes of this story!

They talk about sustainability, clean energy, conservation, and eco-responsibility like they've invented those concepts.

But, like the others, what they've really mastered is nothing more than marketing.

The Green Mask, like many of the other systems we've discussed, is about control. It's about deciding who gets access to what, and at what price. It's about rebranding scarcity as virtue. You're not driving less because the vehicles are putting out more emissions. You're driving less because fuel prices are up, regulations have tightened, and alternatives have been handed out in a way that benefits corporations and governments far more than the planet.

They'll put wind farms on the horizon and solar panels on rooftops while ignoring the mining disasters that pull the lithium and cobalt out of the ground. They'll show you footage of happy workers installing clean tech, but they won't show you the child labor in another country where they're digging it all up with their bare hands so your battery can hold a charge.

The supply chain is "green," but if you follow it to its roots, it's a different kind of green than you think.

The cost of "going green" is always passed down to you. Electric cars only have tax incentives for the upper-middle class and the wealthy. Green home upgrades are only possible if you can afford the up-front cost. Energy-efficient appliances will save you money over time but require you to spend more today. The Green Mask tells you it's all about saving the Earth, but it's really about shifting the burden. You'll pay for the planet's health while they keep cashing in.

It's not that the planet doesn't need saving. It certainly does! From us! You can see the trash in the ocean. You can smell the pollution in the air after a hot summer day. You can watch forests burn year after year while politicians give speeches instead of planting more trees. But the people running The Green Mask have no real interest in solving the problem. Because if the problem gets solved, the control disappears. And they need that control more than the Earth needs clean oceans.

Look at carbon credits…

Sounds noble, right? A way for big polluters to offset their damage by funding green projects. In reality, it's a pay-to-pollute program. If you can afford the credits, you can keep on burning, dumping, and destroying as long as someone plants a few trees on paper. It's like paying someone to clean up your mess while you keep making the same mess every day.

Or take the bans on plastic straws. They get the headlines, the hashtags, the photo ops. Meanwhile, commercial fishing operations dump literally tons of plastic nets and gear into the oceans every year, far more damaging than every straw you've ever used combined. But *you're* the problem! *You're* the one told to sip your drink through paper that falls apart before you finish the drink!

The Green Mask thrives on guilt. You're made to feel like you're killing the planet with every mile you drive, every burger you eat, every plastic wrapper you throw away. And while you're feeling bad about yourself, the same corporations pushing the guilt on you are making the real messes. They've outsourced the blame so you'll quietly carry it for them.

Convenient, isn't it?

And don't think for a minute that they won't weaponize this guilt when it comes to resources. Water is next. As droughts become more common, you'll see water rationing, water meters, and "water rights" traded like commodities. Corporations will own the rights to lakes and rivers, selling the very essence of life back to you at a profit. But it'll be framed as "necessary for conservation." And you'll be the bad guy if you resist any of it.

The Green Mask doesn't want a self-sufficient population. A truly sustainable society would rely less on central systems and less on large-scale control. That would mean communities managing their own resources, generating their own power, producing their own food. But The Green Mask sells just the opposite. You're told to buy into massive renewable grids instead of local solutions. You're told to depend on global supply chains for your "eco-friendly" goods. You're told the right way to save the planet is to keep spending money in the same direction, only with a new label.

Even the language is designed to keep you in line. "Carbon footprint" is a perfect example. It puts the responsibility on you as an individual, as if you alone are tipping the scales of climate change. But your personal "footprint" is a fraction of a fraction compared to that of the top polluting industries! If those industries didn't exist in their current form, your footprint would barely even register. Yet here you are, told to carry the shame like it's your cross to bear.

Mmm, mmm, mmm…

They will never say this out loud, but the Green Mask needs this crisis. It needs the fear. It needs the constant reminder that without them, the world is doomed. They'll let the planet inch toward the edge of collapse if it means they can keep selling the rope they claim will pull it back. It's not about saving the Earth. It never has been.

It's about saving their position.

None of this means you shouldn't care about the environment. That's not what I'm saying. You absolutely should care. But you should care enough to see through this mask they wear. Enough to ask who profits from every "solution" they put in front of you. Care enough to notice that the ones talking the loudest about saving the planet are often the ones who own the industries doing the most damage.

If you want to protect the planet, start small and local. Grow something in your own yard or on your balcony. Support farmers who aren't poisoning the soil. Buy less and waste less, not because they told you to, but because it's the right thing to do. Share resources with your community. Build systems that can't be easily bought or taken away. Because The Green Mask will not save you. It will sell you the illusion of salvation while it cashes your checks.

The real tragedy is that they've turned something as vital and urgent as environmental protection into another arm of control. And every time you buy into their version of "saving the planet" without looking deeper, you tighten the mask over your own face.

So What Now?

Take the mask off.

Stop believing that the only path forward is the one they've paved with recycled slogans and green-tinted lies.

Build your own path, one that doesn't need their permission or their products. And make damn sure your kids know the difference between real care for the Earth and the kind they sell in glossy brochures.

Because the day we stop mistaking control for care is the day The Green Mask falls off the face of the planet for good.

Chapter 22

The Tipping Point

Every major turning point in history has one thing in common…

It's not the invention itself that changes the world. It's the people who control it.

When fire was first discovered, it was something that could cook your food or burn cities to the ground. When the printing press was developed, it could either spread the truth or spread propaganda. Nuclear power could light up the night or level entire cities. The technology itself was never good or bad. It was honestly just neutral. The danger came from the hands that were holding the switch.

We're standing in front of the next great switch.

Artificial Intelligence. The machine that can think, learn, adapt, and act without a human telling it what to do every second.

It won't stay simple, it won't stay limited, and it definitely won't stay in the hands of everyone for very long.

The truth most people don't want to face is that AI is not just a tool, it's a multiplier. If the person holding the keys is good, it can make good things happen much faster, smarter, and at a scale we've never seen before. But if the person holding the keys is corrupt, it will do harm with the same speed and precision.

There will be no middle ground.

Right now, as I write this, the race is on to claim those keys. Governments, corporations, defense contractors, and tech giants are all pouring billions into it. They'll say it's to make your life easier. They'll tell you it's to help the sick, feed the hungry, or educate the poor. And sure, those things might even happen in the beginning, but the deeper goal is *control.* Whoever builds the most advanced AI and locks it behind their walls will eventually own the future.

AI could become the ultimate enforcer.

Imagine a system that never sleeps, never hesitates, and never questions its orders. A system that can predict what you'll do before you even do it. Not because it can read your mind, but because it analyzes every word you've typed, every purchase you've made, every step you've taken, and every conversation you've had in range of a microphone. That's not science fiction. That's already possible. The only thing missing is the scale and the green light to use it.

With the wrong hands on the controls, AI will decide what you see, what you hear, and what you can do. It will monitor everything, down to the smallest detail. It will predict crimes before they happen and label people as risks based on an algorithm. And once a machine decides you're a threat, there will be no one left to argue your case to. No human to convince. Just a line of code that says you're done.

And don't even bet on the "good guys" remaining good, either. Programmers and founders with noble intentions get bought out, pressured, or convinced that compromise is leadership. The same people writing the code today can hand the keys to whoever pays the most tomorrow. Idealism folds fast when money, politics, or fear lean on it hard enough.

But AI doesn't have to be the lock.

It could be the key.

In the right hands, it could break apart these systems I've discussed here that have kept people chained for centuries. It could destroy bureaucracy and make governments truly transparent. It could track corruption and stop it before it spreads. It could distribute resources fairly, cut waste, and automate the jobs that grind people into the dirt while giving them the time and freedom to actually live. It could rebuild trust by letting truth rise to the top instead of letting propaganda win the algorithm war.

The problem is that both futures require the same

technology. The same power. The same speed. Which means the outcome depends entirely on who gets there first and how willing they are to share it.

That's the fork in the road we're standing at right now. So, you cannot sit this one out!

Pretending AI is just another passing trend is how you wake up one day with no control over your life and no way to get it back. This is not the same thing as losing your privacy to social media or letting corporations track your spending. Those were small steps toward control. This is the final leap. Once AI is fully integrated into every system we rely on, there will be no going back without starting over completely.

If it's locked away by the few, they will use it to tighten down on everything. Every system spoken of in this book could be reinforced until it becomes unbreakable. The courts, the military, the media, the corporations, the food supply, the environment—every single one could be monitored, automated, and controlled by AI. And when that happens, there will be no weak points left to push back against. The door will be locked forever.

And when that happens, there is no counterbalance. No revolution to outrun it. No uprising that can match its speed. AI does not sleep, does not eat, does not hesitate. It will enforce the will of whoever holds the keys at a scale no human movement can ever touch.

But if it's shared—truly shared—it could dismantle the same systems. Not in decades, but in years. The same predictive power used to track your every move could be used to track corruption and greed. The same automation that could eliminate jobs could also eliminate meaningless labor, freeing people to create, invent, and live without the constant grind. The same intelligence that could be used to censor could be used to uncover the truth faster than lies can spread.

That's why this moment matters more than any before it. Because the balance really is in your hands. Not in the sense that you can personally program the next great AI. But in the sense that you can decide what you will tolerate moving forward.

You can choose to demand transparency, to question every policy, to resist every attempt to lock the code away from public oversight.

But don't think for a second that this decision will be made for you in some grand public debate. It'll be made quietly, behind closed doors, in boardrooms and government offices. By the time you hear about it, the key could already be gone.

Which means you have to pay attention **now**! Before the choice is made without you.

This is The Tipping Point. The moment where everything could get better… or far, far worse. We've been here before in history, but never with something this powerful. The printing press changed who had access to knowledge. AI will change who has access to control itself.

The question is not whether AI will shape the future. It's already doing that.

The question is whether that future will be an open door… or a locked cell.

If you want the door open, you cannot sit back and trust the people who profit from closed doors. You cannot keep your head down and hope for the best. You have to fight for it now, with your voice, your attention, and your refusal to give them a free pass!

Because if we get this one wrong, there will be no second chance.

There is no "So What Now."

There is only what you do before the door slams shut.

Chapter 23

The Mirror

We can point fingers all day long. At the government, the corporations, the billionaires, the media. They all deserve their share of the blame for how this system is, right?

But the truth that we've been avoiding this whole time is staring us all in the face.

We ourselves have been a major part of the problem too!

That's the thing about these systems. They don't just run on laws and policies alone. They run on compliance. And compliance isn't just signing a form or paying a tax. It's the thousand little ways you've gone along with it, even when you knew it was wrong to do so.

Every time you stayed quiet to keep the peace. Every time you voted for the "lesser evil" and told yourself it was a strategic move. Every time you saw something broken and said, "That's just the way it is."

The Mirror doesn't lie. You've had to make trades along the way. Maybe you've traded truth for comfort, freedom for convenience, integrity for survival. And maybe you told yourself you had no choice. But at some point, you stopped fighting to find one, didn't you?

It's easy to believe the world is broken because "they" broke it. It's harder to admit you've played a role in keeping it that way. But, *you* were the one who bought the products. *You* were the one who clicked the headlines. *You* were the one who scrolled past the suffering. *You* kept The Grind turning because stopping meant risking everything you've built.

The Mirror doesn't care about your excuses. It only cares about what's real. And the reality is, the systems didn't just capture you. They trained you, and then they taught you what to value, what to fear, and what to ignore. And you went along because the alternative was too scary.

You've laughed at people who said they were "opting out" or "living off-grid." You told yourself they were crazy, unrealistic, unstable, or too extreme. But deep down, you envied their refusal to play the game, didn't you? You envied the courage it took to walk away from the table entirely.

The Mirror forces a question you can't dodge…

Are you willing to keep playing by rules that are rigged against you, just because they're familiar? Or are you ready to start breaking them, even if that means standing alone?

It's not an easy choice. It won't come with a movie soundtrack or any applause. Choosing to live differently might cost you your friends, family, and stability. You might even be mocked, dismissed, or even erased from peoples lives. But the alternative is looking into this mirror every day and knowing that you're complicit in your own captivity.

You can smash the glass and pretend you never saw it. Or you can stare into it until the lies burn away and only the truth remains.

The world won't change because you post the right quote or join the right group. It'll change when enough people decide that their reflection isn't good enough anymore, and they do something about it.

So stop looking away. Stop trying to deny your part in this. Let the mirror cut you if it has to. Because the truth is, it's not just them we have to fight…

…It's you.

Chapter 24

The Silence

Silence isn't always the same thing as peace.

Silence, in this system, is what's left when your voice has been beaten out of you. It's the empty space left after they've taken your fight, and your will, and replaced it with the illusion that everything is fine.

But they never take your freedom all at once. They take it in tiny little pieces so that you barely even notice it. A new policy here. A new regulation there. A camera on the street corner you walk past every day. A phrase you avoid saying at work because it "might be taken the wrong way." One day you're speaking your mind, and the next you're calculating every word before it leaves your mouth.

That's the real trick that most people don't consider. They don't have to be the "thought police" from Orwell's book "1984" if they can train you to police yourself.

The systems have been building toward this for decades. They call it "safety," and "order." They tell you that free speech comes with "responsibility," and that "responsibility" means never saying anything that makes someone in power uncomfortable. You can't argue with the rules because the rules are written in a language that sounds reasonable… until you realize it's just code for keeping you quiet.

People think silence comes from fear of punishment. That's only half of the truth. The deeper silence comes from exhaustion. You get tired of fighting. Tired of being the one who speaks up and gets shut down, mocked, or ignored. You get tired of feeling like the crazy one in the room just because you refuse to nod along. Again, ask me how I know.

So, little by little… you stop.

The systems know this. They know it better than you know yourself. They've studied it, gamed it, perfected it. They know how far to push you before you burn out, and they make sure to stretch the fight just long enough to drain you without completely bleeding you out. Because a broken person might rebel, but a tired person will just go home and keep quiet.

This is how entire generations disappear into compliance. The battles you thought would define you fade into background noise. The fire in your chest turns into a small, dim glow… just enough to keep you alive, but not enough to light anything else. You call it "picking and choosing your battles," but the truth is, they've taught you to stop choosing any battles at all.

The Silence is not an accident. It's a system in itself. It's the final stage of control. When they no longer have to force you to obey, but you just do anyway. Not because you agree, but because you've been worn down to the point where agreement and survival feel like the same thing.

And the most dangerous part is, you start telling yourself it's better this way. You start believing that speaking up isn't worth it. You tell yourself, "things aren't that bad," or "someone else will fight that fight." You start playing the same script that's been fed to you your whole damn life, and you don't even notice when the words coming out of your mouth aren't even yours anymore.

This is the moment they've been building towards. The point where control becomes invisible. Where the bars are gone, but you still stay in the cage because you've forgotten how to leave.

The truth is, The Silence spreads faster than the noise does. One person shuts up, and the people around them take the hint. Conversations stop. Questions vanish. Opinions become whispers you only share with people you already agree with. Soon, the only voices left are the ones repeating what the system wants you to hear.

By the time you notice it, it's too late. The walls have already closed in on you.

But The Silence is not a void. It's more like a pressure. It grows heavier the longer you live with it. And one day, you wake up and realize you've been holding your breath

…for years.

So what now?

You don't get to stay quiet anymore.

Every time you bite your tongue, every time you "let it slide," every time you trade your voice for comfort, you're helping The Silence spread.

You're building the very walls that trap you… and everyone else.

Stop waiting for someone braver to speak first. There's no one coming! It's you! It's always been you!

Say the things they don't want said. Ask the questions they hope you never ask. Refuse the script, even if your voice shakes when you do it. That's how it breaks, with one voice at a time, refusing to shut up!

Because if you don't speak, nothing changes. Not for you. Not for anyone. And make no mistake… the system is counting on that!

The only thing stronger than their control is your refusal to play along. The longer you wait, the tighter the grip gets.

So speak! Speak when it's uncomfortable, when it costs you, when they tell you it's better to keep quiet.

Because if you stay silent, you've already surrendered.

Chapter 25

The Return

At some point along the way, the fog begins to clear. You see the systems for what they are… and you see yourself inside them. You see the strings, the levers, the endless patterns meant to keep you quiet, obedient, and small. And then it hits you that this isn't just how things are, this is how they've been created to be.

You see how it's been this way for *so long*.

You never stood outside the system and looked in. You were born into it, shaped by it, fed by it, and steered by it. Your fears, your dreams, your opinions, even the way you speak to your friends at dinner. All of these pieces of you have been programmed without your consent.

And you let it happen because you didn't know any better.

But now you know.

And once you see it, my hope is that you won't be able to forget it. There's no going back to the comfortable sleep where your compliance is really just safety.

That world is gone now.

Let it go.

Now you face a choice: Do you drift back into the quiet slumber? Or do you take yourself back, piece by piece, inch by inch, from the machine that's been feeding on your silence?

This isn't about overthrowing governments or lighting the streets on fire. That shit doesn't change anything! This has to start much smaller than that.

And it starts with you refusing to live as someone else's puppet…

You begin by questioning everything you were taught to accept without thought. You stop swallowing their headlines whole. You stop repeating the talking points that were designed to divide you. You stop apologizing for having your own mind. You decide, right here and right now, that you will no longer confuse survival with submission.

Taking your life back won't happen in a single moment of rebellion. It happens the same way they took it from you to begin with, piece by piece, choice by choice. They chipped away at you slowly. Now you have to chip away at the falsity until you find the real you that's been hiding under all of it.

You start paying attention to what you consume,

because everything you allow into your mind and body shapes the world you see and your reactions to it. You start watching who benefits from your fear, your outrage, your loyalty, and your silence.

It will *definitely* be uncomfortable! Trust me. You will lose people too. Probably many. You'll find yourself in rooms where you're the only one who sees, the only one who doesn't play along. They'll mock you, question you, and try to pull you back into The Script, because your refusal forces them to face their own silence.

Let them.

You weren't built to fit into their box. You were built to choose, to think, to decide for yourself who you are and what you stand for. That's your Return. Not to who you were before you saw the truth, but to the person underneath all of the conditioning.

Freedom doesn't mean walking away from every system. It means refusing to let the systems define you. It means reclaiming your voice when they told you to shut up. It means remembering the fire in your chest before they convinced you to dim it down. It means learning, over and over, that you are not theirs to control.

And it's going to take work! Real work. The kind that burns away parts of you.

You'll have to rebuild your confidence from the ground up after years of being told to stay quiet. You'll have to confront the part of you that wanted the comfort of compliance. You'll have to fight your own exhaustion and the constant temptation to lay your head back down and pretend you never woke up.

Because waking up is hard! But *staying* awake is *much* harder!

The systems are counting on you faltering. They know how many people will see the strings and choose to look away. They know how many will decide that it's too much, too risky, too lonely to question what's always been accepted. That's why they always win. Not because they're stronger, but because they're patient. They wait for you… until you give up.

So, don't give up!

You don't need anyone's permission to question the world you live in. You don't need a title, a platform, or a movement behind you. Your power is in refusing to be quiet.

The return is not about fixing the system. It's about fixing yourself. The systems have been here for centuries. They'll evolve, mutate, and disguise themselves as something new. But you, the individual, you can decide right now that you will no longer feed them with your silence.

That's the key.

The moment you stop playing their game, they lose their grip on you.

They want you obedient. They want you distracted. They want you tired enough to give up.

Do not give them what they want!

So what now?

Speak!

Speak up even when your voice shakes. Speak when they tell you to sit down and shut up. Speak when everyone around you has convinced themselves it's safer to stay silent.

Stop outsourcing your mind. Stop waiting for someone else to fight your battles. Stop living on a script that was handed to you by people who profit from your compliance.

Start with one decision. One refusal. One moment where you choose honesty over comfort. Then another. And another. And another…

The Return begins the moment you decide you're done living small. The moment you remember that your voice matters. The moment that you choose, fully and without apology, to live like you belong to yourself.

Because the truth is simple…

If you don't speak, you've already been spoken for.

And that's what they thrive on.

Chapter 26

The Shift

Lets assume that you've taken your life back from the systems as much as you can.

Piece by piece. Hour by hour...

Well, I hate to say it, but that's not the end of the fight... it's actually just the foundation for the next one.

The Return was about reclaiming your ground.

The Shift is about moving it.

Here's the thing... You cannot stay free for long inside a machine that was built to pull you back in. You can work hard, keep your head down, and build something honest, but the systems will still be there. It'll keep nudging, taxing, regulating, and redirecting you until you're right back where you started.

Let me make this perfectly clear up front... what I'm about to say isn't about chasing a perfect society in any way, shape or form. Utopias are like fragile glass bubbles that shatter the second reality taps them. This is about building something durable. Something practical. Something rooted in human nature, not wishful thinking.

The Shift is about reshaping the way we live so that survival doesn't require submission to the old systems.

So...

We start small. Not because small is safe, but because small is how you plant something that lasts. You don't rip the old world out of the ground and try to replace it immediately. You starve it, bit by bit, while building something stronger right beside it. That means creating systems of our own that people can actually live in. Not with fancy slogans, or new committees, but with real, functional replacements for the ones that keep us trapped.

The first step is changing the main question...

Stop asking, "How do we fix what's broken?" and start asking, "How do we make this broken system irrelevant?" You cannot reform a structure designed to keep you in your place. You have to give people a door out of it and make that door too good to ignore.

That proverbial door begins with meeting basic needs in ways that don't require playing by the system's rules. Food, water, shelter, energy, and meaningful work are the pillars. As long as you depend entirely on the system for any one of those, you'll have to trade obedience for access. If you can meet even one of them outside their reach, you'll have a small amount of leverage.

Start where you are...

If it's food, you plant it. Even a single raised bed in a backyard or a shared garden between neighbors is a start. You don't wait for land reform or policy changes. You grow something now, even if it's small. If it's housing, you learn repair skills. You make a home last instead of feeding the constant churn of the housing market. If it's energy, you invest in something as simple as a small solar setup that can keep essential devices running during an outage.

These are not luxuries.

These are *exits!*

Then comes the step most people overlook. You share the skill, not just the result. When you can grow your own lettuce, you teach the neighbor who asked about it. When you can fix a leaky pipe, you let someone watch and learn. When you can keep a computer running with secondhand parts, you show someone else how to do it. A single self-reliant person is an anomaly. A collection of them is a **Shift**.

The next layer is cooperation. We're not talking about charity, nor handouts, but real exchange that reduces everyone's need for the old system. If your neighbor grows tomatoes and you have eggs, you trade. If someone in your circle can weld and another can sew, you start building an informal network of skills and goods. It doesn't need a name or a logo. It just needs consistency and trust. The more you can create a loop that meets needs without money changing hands, the less dependent you become on the machine that prints the money.

This will not be neat and tidy! At first, it may feel small and scattered. That's fine. You're laying groundwork, and groundwork is not glamorous. The point is not to build an instant alternative to the entire system. The point is to prove, one piece at a time, that you can live without feeding it as much as you used to.

From here, you scale it in ways that keep integrity intact. If a group in your area grows enough food to have a surplus, you set up a local exchange. If you have more tools than you use, you create a lending system (think of a tool library). The idea is to replace competition with collaboration so that more people have enough.

The Shift is not about winning arguments with the system. It's about making the system's rules less and less relevant until they no longer define the game. You'll still have to engage with it in some ways. Taxes will still exist. Regulations will still exist. But the goal is to be able to say no when those rules cross your line. The power you'll gain only comes from not needing them for everything.

And here's where the fear kicks in for most people. "What if it fails?" "What if no one else joins in?" "What if it's too hard?" The truth is, it will fail in small ways at first. People will quit. Some will take more than they give. The first garden might get wiped out by a bad drought. The first tool library might lose half its inventory to selfishness. It will be hard! That doesn't mean the vision is broken. It means the learning curve is real.

Everything worth having has a cost.

The Shift is not an overnight migration. It's simply a

slow transfer of the weight. You keep one foot in the old world because you have to, but you start putting more and more of your life into the new one you're building. You might begin with five percent outside the system. Then it becomes ten. Then twenty. The more you shift, the harder it becomes for the old rules to pull you back.

This is where you have to resist the temptation to brand it, politicize it, or turn it into a single movement with leaders and spokespeople. That's the hardest part. But it's one of the most important ones! Movements get infiltrated. Leaders get corrupted. Keep it local. Keep it rooted in relationships, **not in hierarchy!** A thousand independent pockets of resilience are harder to dismantle than one big organization. Don't return back to the old ways of doing things just because it gets difficult sometimes.

By the time The Shift reaches a tipping point, the system will start to notice. It'll try to pull people back with convenience, fear, and incentives. That's when the work of the earlier stages (hopefully) pays off. If you and your network can meet your needs without their help, those offers will feel less tempting at that point. The only way this vision works is if the alternative you build is not just ethical in nature, but better all the way around in practice.

And remember, this is not a utopia, and certainly not "communism" as I'm sure it will be labled. It's not something meant to be perfect. People will still disagree. Some will still cheat and steal. Mistakes will still happen. The goal is not to create a flawless society but a freer one.

One where your survival and dignity are not tied to your willingness to be managed.

The Shift is the bridge between taking your life back and building a future that doesn't need the system at all. It's the phase where ideas become infrastructure and personal independence becomes collective strength. It's messy, it's slow, and it's worth every ounce of effort. Because once enough people have crossed that bridge, there will be no going back.

Chapter 27

The Framework

You really can't rebuild anything without a foundation to hold it up, right? Momentum without direction will cause burn out. Good intentions without a plan will turn into another forgotten movement. The Return you've made to yourself in the last few chapters is the fuel, but The Framework is the engine that runs it all once The Shift begins to take place.

The Framework is the part that most people skip because it's not glamorous. It's not a rally in the streets or some viral video. It's the blueprint for how we will live, work, and share resources in a way that isn't just another system that's waiting to rot from the inside.

As I stated in the previous chapter, it starts small. Always. The foundation of a sustainable future isn't written in the halls of government or in the boardrooms of billionaires. It begins in the neighborhoods, towns, and cities where people choose to work together with a clear purpose. Not through charity, not through dependence, but through collaboration.

The first layer is local self-reliance. You look at the basics of survival—food, water, shelter, energy—and then you start producing as much of them as possible within walking distance of where people live. Rooftop gardens. Community greenhouses. Shared rainwater systems. Local energy grids powered by solar, wind, or micro-hydro. These aren't just eco-friendly feel-good projects. They're insurances against the fragility of global supply chains.

The second layer is skill integration. Every community already has untapped skill sets scattered throughout its people. Carpenters. Programmers. Gardeners. Plumbers. Teachers. Mechanics. The Framework puts those skills into a shared pool where they can be used for collective benefit before they can be sold to the highest bidder. You create a local exchange, not with monopoly money or "credits" that mimic the same broken economic system we're trying to replace, but with agreements and trust backed by visible results.

This is where technology, especially AI, becomes an amplifier instead of a threat. Imagine an AI that maps every skill in a community, matches them to needs in real time, and predicts upcoming shortages before they happen. AI that doesn't just serve ads or mines data, but runs logistics for food distribution, energy balancing, and education scheduling. The tech already exists. The difference is in whose hands are on it and who/what it's trained to serve.

The third layer is infrastructure for shared tools and spaces. Not everyone needs to own every tool available. The Framework creates communal workshops, shared transportation hubs, cooperative kitchens, and storage networks. It's cheaper, more efficient, and keeps wealth in the community instead of bleeding it into corporate pockets. AI could streamline this too, making sure those tools are booked, maintained, and available when needed. No different than how streaming platforms manage digital libraries, but for real-world goods.

The fourth layer is production with purpose. This means moving away from producing for profit alone and toward producing for human needs first. Local manufacturing hubs using small-scale automation, 3D printing, and repurposed machinery can make everything from furniture to replacement parts. With AI-assisted design and fabrication, turnaround can be fast, waste will be minimal, and reliance on outside suppliers eventually drops.

The fifth layer is education that adapts to reality. Forget the one-size-fits-all curriculum's. In The Framework, education is continuous, adaptive, and is directly tied to the needs and goals of the community. AI tutors can deliver custom learning plans to every individual, not to create test-takers, but to create problem-solvers who can keep the new systems running and evolving.

Now, the question most people ask: How do you get

from here to there without tearing everything down first? The answer is "staged transition." You don't start by demanding that people abandon their jobs or the currency system overnight. You create parallel structures that work alongside the existing ones, giving people a choice. At first, they participate in both worlds. Over time, as The Framework proves it can meet more needs, reliance on the old systems fades naturally.

Step one: Pilot Communities. A single neighborhood, small town, or even a city block starts implementing these layers in miniature. Document everything! What works, what doesn't, what resources were hardest to secure? AI can track and analyze every variable, learning from failures and then replicating successes in the next location faster and cheaper.

Step two: Connect the pilots. Once you have a handful of functioning hubs, you start linking them together, not with bureaucracy, but with agreements on resource sharing and skill exchanges. Each community remains self-reliant but gains the strength of being part of a larger network. If one hub's water system fails, another can supply it temporarily. If one area is rich in solar energy, it can send surplus to others.

Step three: Widen the reach. As more people see the stability and freedom that comes from The Framework, adoption begins to grow. AI can project demand, identify expansion points, and prevent bottlenecks before they happen.

This is important! So pay attention! The growth is

supposed to be intentional, not explosive!

Step four: Cultural integration. This is where the shift becomes self-sustaining. Kids grow up seeing resource-sharing as normal. Adults see self-reliance as a given, not a fringe lifestyle. The idea of paying for basic survival starts to feel absurd.

The key to all of this is a different type of control. Not top-down, but distributed. Decisions aren't made by a central authority. They're made locally, by the people directly affected, with AI acting as an unbiased data tool rather than a ruler. This removes the fragility of central failure and the corruption that comes with concentrated power.

This is not a dream that requires everyone to be enlightened saints, either. It works because it removes scarcity as a weapon. It works because it's cheaper to collaborate than to compete for the essentials. It works because technology, when guided by human values instead of corporate greed, can handle the complexity of managing shared resources without the waste of our current systems.

We are not waiting for governments to approve this. We are not asking billionaires to fund it. We are building it ourselves, from scratch! Because the alternative is waiting for collapse and hoping to survive the fallout. That doesn't make much sense to me. The Framework is the lifeboat we start rowing now, so we're not begging for rescue later.

AI is going to be part of the future whether we like it

or not. The choice is whether it becomes the perfect prison guard or the perfect builder's tool. In this Framework, it's the latter. It doesn't replace human hands or human decisions. It frees them. It takes the administrative grind, the scheduling, the optimization, and the forecasting off our backs so we can put our time into what only we can do… create, repair, mentor, grow, and connect.

The Framework is not an escape from reality. It's reality rebuilt in a way that makes sense. The pieces already exist. The skills already exist. The tech already exists. The only missing piece is the decision to stop waiting for permission.

When enough communities choose to start, The Framework stops being a theory and instead becomes the backbone of a new way to live. And once you've built a life on a foundation like that, you'll never look back.

Let's get started.

Chapter 28

The Rebuild

You wake up without an alarm. The sunlight is your clock, and your body's rhythm is your guide. There's no rush to beat traffic, no inbox full of "urgent" messages waiting to steal your morning.

You step outside and the air *feels* different. Cleaner. Fresher. Not because someone sent out a new memo on emissions, but because the systems that once pumped waste into the skies aren't running for profit anymore. They're running for life. The streets are quiet except for the sound of people walking, kids laughing, the hum of machines built to serve the community instead of a stock price.

Again, we're not talking about a utopia. This isn't perfect. People still get sick, mistakes still happen, storms still roll in and knock things down and blow things around. But the difference is, here, in this system, those things aren't made worse by the weight of an outdated machine that feeds on scarcity and fear. Problems are met with solutions, not price tags. Challenges are faced together instead of becoming someone's business model.

Work, as you once knew it, doesn't exist here. The endless grind of selling your hours to buy back your survival with paper is gone. People still work of course, but not out of fear of losing their home or feeding their family. The work is chosen, not coerced. You take on the roles you're good at, the ones that feel meaningful to you, and your contribution meets the needs of others just as theirs meet yours.

Food isn't locked behind a price tag. It's grown locally in stacked greenhouses, vertical farms, rooftop gardens, and community plots. You can pick it yourself, or you can have it delivered by autonomous transport. Nobody counts how many apples you take, because the orchard produces more than enough for everyone. Nobody's hoarding oranges because there's no shortage. Scarcity isn't engineered here. Abundance is.

Energy is silent. No smokestacks. No wires draped across every street. Solar, wind, tidal, and geothermal power hum in the background. Your home runs on what the Earth gives freely, and your community stores enough to share during cloudy days and windless nights.

Healthcare isn't a privilege. It's a resource, like water or sunlight. You don't "apply" for it, you don't "qualify" for it, you just walk in and get what you need. The person treating you isn't watching the clock or fighting insurance codes. They're focused on healing you because they enjoy healing people.

Education is open to everyone at every age. Want to learn astrophysics at sixty? Go for it. Want to become a carpenter at fifteen? Start tomorrow. Nobody holds the keys to knowledge that's been locked behind a payment plan, because the point isn't to create a competitive advantage, it's to create a competent, capable, connected human race.

There's no advertising here. No billboards telling you you're not enough. No pop-up ads begging you to click. The streets aren't littered with messages designed to manipulate you. Instead, walls are covered in art. Murals tell the history of the people who live here. Interactive boards share community updates, upcoming projects, and opportunities to contribute. The noise is gone, and in its place is only clarity.

The word "job" has been replaced with "role" (not to be mistaken for "The Role") and this new role changes as your life does. You might help with food production for a few years, then design housing, then teach music. Your value isn't in how much profit you can make for someone else. It's in how much life you can bring to the table.

In this future, "success" isn't measured by bank accounts. It's measured by wellness, connection, and contribution. If your neighbor's roof needs fixing, you help fix it. If the school needs more materials, they're printed on-site within the hour. The question isn't "Who will pay for it?" The question is "Do we have the resources?" And if the answer is yes, then the work begins immediately.

Money doesn't vanish here overnight. It simply fades as we build systems that make it irrelevant. When everything you need is freely available because it's been produced efficiently and sustainably, the power of money to control you evaporates.

This world didn't appear by magic. It came to be because people refused to keep rebuilding the old system every time the flaws were glaring at them. They chose to build something entirely different instead. Something designed around access instead of ownership, contribution instead of competition, and cooperation instead of coercion.

Stand here long enough in this vision, and you'll notice something odd. The constant low-level anxiety you've carried your whole life isn't there anymore. You're not bracing for the next bill, the next emergency, or the next stock market crash. You're free to think about bigger things. Not just surviving the week, but shaping the world around you.

You can walk through your neighborhood and see people solving problems without waiting for permission. A broken water pipe is fixed within minutes because someone knew how and had what they needed to do it. A community hall is built because enough hands wanted it to exist. A playground is expanded because a few parents noticed the kids had outgrown the old one. Elder parents and grandparents are cared for in their own homes because there's no longer a profit motive to send them away.

None of it's perfect, by any means. Sometimes projects take longer than planned. Sometimes resources run low and people have to rethink their approach. Sometimes personalities clash. But here, those setbacks aren't excuses to give up. They're chances to adapt and get smarter together.

I can't emphasize this enough…this is not a perfect world! And it never claims to be. It's simply a better way. One that accepts human flaws but refuses to let them be the foundation for an entire economy. One that plans for resilience instead of constant rescue. One that believes life isn't supposed to be a musical chairs competition to see who can take the most before the music stops.

The Rebuild is a choice. It's not a dream you wait for. It's a design you start building before the old world collapses under its own weight. And the longer you stand here in this vision, the more you realize it's not only possible.

It's absolutely necessary.

Chapter 29

The Exit

There's a point in many stories where the main character can't go back to where he or she came from. It usually isn't because the path is blocked, but because they've changed too much to fit back into the life they've left behind.

That's where you are right now.

You've walked through the darkness, seen the systems for what they are, and felt the weight of knowing there's no one coming to save you. You've seen the tipping points, the mirrors, the frameworks. You've seen that the collapse isn't something to fear, it's something to prepare for… because it's already in motion.

And now you're standing in the doorway.

The Exit.

Here's the thing about exits: they're not always marked.

Sometimes they're a broken fence at the back of a field. Sometimes they're a side road no one else notices. Sometimes they're a path so small that everyone else misses it until it's too late. But you've learned to see them now.

The Exit is not a place. It's a rejection. A refusal to give your energy to the systems that grind you down. A refusal to buy into the stories you now know are lies. A refusal to be part of the machine unless you're the one using it to build something worth keeping.

This isn't about disappearing into the woods, cutting ties with the world, or becoming some caricature of "off-grid rebellion." Although you're certainly free to do that if you wish. It's about no longer feeding the very thing that keeps the majority of us weak. It's about placing your energy where it grows life, not where it fuels control.

You've already started. Every time you've questioned a rule that didn't make sense. Every time you've stopped giving your money to companies that exploit. Every time you've turned away from propaganda instead of arguing with it. Every time you've chosen to create something instead of endlessly consuming. Those were all exits in miniature. You didn't call them that at the time… but that's what they were.

Now you're being asked to make it intentional. Permanent. Not a momentary break from the system, but a new operating mode altogether. One where you don't look to the old powers for permission, approval, or for salvation.

Unfortunately, you won't be able to take everyone with you. Some people will never walk through that door with you. Some will laugh at the idea of leaving. Some will dismiss it as "Communism" (Ha!) and never consider it again. Others will feel the pull but then freeze at the threshold. That's their choice. Yours is to move forward without waiting for their permission.

The truth is, you've been exiting in pieces for a while now. Every time you questioned what you were told, every time you chose truth over comfort, every time you put your energy into building something instead of begging for scraps. That's what's gotten you to this point.

This is the final piece:

You have to stop looking back.

The old systems will keep screaming for your attention. They'll try to lure you back with fear, nostalgia, or false promises. But you already know the ending to that story. You've lived it for far too long.

So…

This is not the part where I hand you a "what now?" There is no what now anymore. There's only doing it or not doing it. Building or watching it burn. Walking through The Exit or standing in the doorway until the building comes down around you.

You've got the truth now. You've got the tools. You've got the clarity. Whether you act on it is the only decision left to make.

The door is open.

Walk.

Epilogue

The Choice

You've made it to the end, but this isn't the end.

Not really, anyway.

If you've read this far, you've walked through the systems with me. You've seen the weight they place on us, the quiet ways they shape us, and the hidden machinery beneath what we were taught to think of as "normal." Maybe some of it shook you. Maybe some of it just confirmed what you've always felt but couldn't explain. Either way, you've seen more than most people ever will.

And now you're standing at this unusual crossroads.

You can put this book down, slip back into the current, and let the system carry you where it wants you to go. Or you can choose to step outside of it, deliberately, and in your own time.

This book wasn't written for tearing everything down.

It's not about chaos or rebellion for the sake of rebellion. It's simply about awareness. It's about remembering that you are more than the roles they've trained you to play. More than your job, your possessions, your opinions, or your place in someone else's hierarchy. It's about taking back the one thing they've been trying to keep you from your entire life:

Yourself.

You don't need to fight every battle. You don't need to save the world. But you do need to decide who you're going to be in it. The Choice is yours now… and it always has been.

So pause here for a moment. Take a breath. Look around you at the people, the systems, the distractions, the noise. And then look inward. Ask yourself who you are without all of it, and who you're willing to become.

Because after everything we've walked through together, there's only one truth left to hold on to:

The systems may shape the world around you, but they don't get to define you.

That part has always been yours.

About the Author

I've spent most of my life working in the trades and running small businesses. Nothing glamorous, just the kind of work that keeps a roof over your head and food on the table.

Along the way, I started paying attention to the systems around me…money, politics, education, religion, and how much they shape us, whether we realize it or not.

I didn't write this book as an expert looking down on anyone. I'm not an "expert" at anything. I wrote it as someone who's lived inside the same systemic crap you have, someone who's watched how the rules are set up and how they keep people stuck in an endless loop.

I don't claim to have all the answers. What I do know is that things don't have to stay the way they are, and asking the hard questions about where we go from here is the first step toward changing them.

Thank you for making it to the end of this book. I hope to see you again in the new and improved world we have yet to create!

If this book meant something to you, I'd appreciate a kind review. It helps more than you know!

www.ingramcontent.com/pod-product-compliance
Lightning Source LLC
Chambersburg PA
CBHW061448150726
47987CB00001B/375